Statements from Allies

Keith Strickland's book is  show how adults can provi cation, preparation, affirn help youth empower thems richer lives. Many young people are confined by mental chains. For some, that state of mind is just as devastating as being behind bars. The author is an authority on the subject matter. I am proud to acknowledge that my mentee, as an ex-offender, has written a detailed roadmap to help our children navigate life.

—Karla Winfrey
Emmy Award–Winning Multimedia Journalist

I met a true public servant leader when I met Keith Strickland. God wants our lives to overflow with mercy, love, and compassion—the marks of His kingdom. We have a choice: respond to the unsettling realities of this world with fear and avoidance or respond to the greatest needs of the people in this world with love, hope, and tender loving care. God encourages us to imitate the Faithful Servant, and Keith Strickland shows us how to be that faithful servant through his service to youth and those who are incarcerated.

Keith Strickland shows us how to truly love each other even when we do not really know each other. Keith uses his time, energy, attention, affection, resources, and money to care for and love others. When we are blessed to be connected with a servant like Keith Strickland, we must know that as much as he cares for others, we need to care for him.

1 Corinthians 13: 13 (NIV) says, "And now these three remain: faith, hope and love. But the greatest of these is love." Keith is the greatest example of love.

—Natalie Hall
Fulton County Commissioner

The power of true leadership is very rare in times like these. Keith Strickland is an altruistic, charitable, and generous humanitarian. Keith fights for the opportunities for the have-nots to have. As a legislator in the Georgia General Assembly and as the chair of the Georgia Legislative Black Caucus, Keith has worked with me for years to ensure successful legislation that has helped underserved Georgians. I am thankful to know Keith, and Georgia is blessed to have such a magnanimous servant.

—Carl Gilliard
State Representative, Savannah, Georgia

Collaborating with Keith Strickland has been one of the paramount highlights of my tenure as a chief school superintendent over the past decade in several school systems. Witnessing Keith's mentorship, weaving hope into the lives of our most vulnerable middle and high school students, evokes a profound awe.

His reservoir of extraordinary compassion, interwoven with humility, and his artistry in sharing the narrative of his own life capture the minds and hearts of young adults who want to become a part of his life. Keith is one of the most critical levers of life transformation for the students I've served, and his story must be told and read by as many others as possible so his impact can extend far beyond its current boundaries.

—Scott Taylor
Superintendent, Township of Union Public Schools

As the district attorney for Rockdale County, I have had the honor of working with Keith Strickland on the implementation of our youth intervention and diversion programs. When Keith and I first met as strangers years ago, our faith, passion, and purpose of saving our youth from the troubles of crime and incarceration immediately connected us. Keith represents the hope and promise of all youth currently wrapped up in the criminal justice system. The fulfillment of his calling underscores the duty of those of us with the platform and power to do so, to invest in the future of who are youth can be—not in the past mistakes they have made. Keith's experiences, insight, and life's work will surely be an inspiration and a call to action to anyone who reads his testimony. I am proud to not only know Keith but to call him a friend.

—Alisha Adams Johnson
District Attorney, Rockdale Judicial Circuit

Youth Change Agent

Youth

Change Agent

EMPOWER A YOUNG PERSON TO MAKE THE TRANSITION TO A BETTER LIFE

Keith Strickland

with Lucas L. Johnson II

Broadleaf Books
Minneapolis

YOUTH CHANGE AGENT
Empower a Young Person to Make the Transition to a Better Life

Library of Congress Cataloging-in-Publication Data
Names: Strickland, Keith, author. | Johnson, Lucas, author.
Title: Youth change agent : empower a young person to make the
    transition to a better life / Keith Strickland, Lucas L. Johnson II.
Description: Minneapolis, MN : Broadleaf Books, [2024]
Identifiers: LCCN 2023045588 (print) | LCCN 2023045589 (ebook) |
    ISBN 9781506495453 (paperback) | ISBN 9781506495460 (ebook)
Subjects: LCSH: At-risk youth—Behavior modification—
    United States. | At-risk youth—Counseling of—United
    States. | Mentoring. | Conduct of life. | Change (Psychology)
Classification: LCC HV1431 .S834 2024 (print) | LCC
    HV1431 (ebook) | DDC 362.74—dc23/eng/20231219
LC record available at https://lccn.loc.gov/2023045588
LC ebook record available at https://lccn.loc.gov/2023045589

Cover design: Richard Tapp

Print ISBN: 978-1-5064-9545-3
eBook ISBN: 978-1-5064-9546-0

This book is dedicated to my daughter in heaven,
everyone who helped me become
the father she deserved, all the friends
who lost their lives along the way, and
all the youth who are still becoming.

Contents

How This Book Began

Throughout my twenty-four years as a reporter with the Associated Press, people approached me with story ideas or individuals I should consider writing about. When Karla Winfrey told me about Keith Strickland, I wanted to hear more. His incredible life story and the much-needed work he's doing made me quickly realize the need for more than just an article.

I approached him about writing a book, and I'm grateful to have had the opportunity to work with him on this project that has inspired me to do even more to help our youth make the transition to better lives.

The fulfillment I get when one of them realizes his or her true potential never gets old. I'm reminded of the words of Marianne Williamson: "Our deepest fear is not that we are inadequate. Our deepest fear is that we are powerful beyond measure. . . . We ask ourselves, who am I to be brilliant, gorgeous, talented, fabulous? Actually, who are you not to be? You are a child of God."

—*Lucas L. Johnson II*

Understanding Why Youth Choose Certain Paths

The greatest good you can do for
another is not just to share your riches,
but to reveal to him his own.

—*Benjamin Disraeli*

It was a Saturday evening, and I had just attended an event to honor the Black legislators for the state of Georgia, which has the highest number of African Americans in state government leadership positions of any state.

I knew many of them personally. We worked in the community together for years. I watched them run for office. I helped them create initiatives like youth crime intervention and prevention programs, community outreach and advocacy projects, criminal justice reform work, and write new policies, among other things. I was honored to be there to salute them, our public servants, who give until they are depleted, but are rarely poured back into. Some of them, emotionally drained, have called me after a terrible bill passed and there was nothing they could do to stop it, no matter how hard they tried. They are not just my friends—they are the soldiers I fight on the battlefield with for justice and equality.

After the event, I headed back to my office. I had work that needed to be finished before the beginning of the next workday. I thought I could spend a few hours in the office, but I ended up working until the sun came up. With everything done, I had one last stop before finally going home and resting. Where I was headed was in walking distance, so I made my way through a parking lot. It had been raining so the ground was wet. Right when I was carefully trying to walk through a muddy area, I heard something behind me. A bit startled, I turned to see what it was and slipped in the mud, then fell onto my back. When I looked up, I saw a young man standing over me with a gun. There was a fierceness in his eyes.

I was being robbed. My main concern at the time was making sure this stayed a robbery—and did not turn into a murder.

"You literally caught me slipping." I was trying to lighten the moment so he wouldn't think I was a threat. Even though a cloth was partly covering his face, I felt like I could not only see him, but I could also see inside of him. I could feel the intensity of his heartbeat. The heat in his breath. The rage in his soul. I wanted to lessen the intensity of the moment.

A scared man could easily pull a trigger unintentionally and leave me dead accidentally. I didn't want him to shoot me by mistake. If he felt threatened, I thought, he might pull the trigger before he even knew it.

He didn't respond. This was not going exactly how he expected. I could tell he didn't know what to say or how to respond to what I said. Inside, I was afraid, but he couldn't see it.

"How are we doing this? What type of robbery is this, King?" I decided to take control and keep everything moving since he did not say anything. The quicker he got what he wanted, the faster I would be back on my feet and gone. The better the odds were that I would leave alive and without any extra holes in my body. "Do you want the money out my pocket, or am I taking off my shoes and watch?" I grew up in rough neighborhoods. This was not my first time being robbed or having a gun pointed at me.

The young man's eyes seemed to darken. "Give me your money!" Even though he did not yell because people were close enough to hear him, if we got too loud, his voice was deeper and more aggressive. The only thing separating us from other people in the parking lot was a thin line of trees. I could tell he was serious and was willing to do whatever he felt he had to. He did not need to raise his voice.

I did not want to push him, but I still wanted to maintain some level of control.

"We can do this three different ways. I can go in my pockets. You can go in my pockets. You can help me up, then go in my pockets." I wanted him to understand I was not resisting, at all. I needed him to tell me what to do and then let me do it. "I don't think you should lean over me to go in my pockets. You have to worry about me pulling you down or falling in the mud." Think of what could happen if he fell in the mud because he lost his balance while still pointing a gun at me!

"I'm not helping you up!" He yelled this time.

I started going in my pockets, so I could give him what he asked for.

"Get your hands out of your pockets!" This time he started to lean toward me, and he pointed the gun closer to my face.

I looked around to see if anyone heard him yell. What I was worried about was just about to happen. "Get behind the tree. Someone's about to walk up." I saw a man with his dog walking in our direction. I tried to warn the young man, but he kept the gun in my face and didn't budge. So, I repeated myself, this time more aggressively. "Get behind the damn tree before the man sees you and calls the police!"

The dog was close enough to hear us by this time. The young man moved behind the tree. When the man saw me, I played it off like I slipped and fell in the mud. The man didn't seem to care very much. He let his dog do what he needed to do, then walked away.

The young man came back out, his gun still pointed at my face. "Why did you—"

Before he could finish, I responded, "All you want is my money. I don't want to see you go to prison or for an old man to get hurt." I started taking my money out.

The young man gave me a different type of look. I could tell he was collecting his thoughts and processing everything that happened. He asked, "Are you Muslim?"

I knew exactly why he asked me. He didn't want to hurt me—as a Muslim man, he was bound to not hurt another Muslim brother. Also, he took the cloth from over his face when he went behind the tree. Maybe he had to remove it to see me clearly, to know if I warned the guy with the dog? Whatever the reason, I saw his face this time.

"I'm not Muslim." I knew saying I was his brother could have saved my life. Jesus died for me. I would rather die claiming Christ than live by denying him.

"But you saw my face." This time, the young man's voice was softer. It was like he was talking to himself, not me.

"All I see is a King doing what he thinks he has to do to survive." I didn't know how he was going to respond, but I was speaking from my heart.

"Why did you help me?" The young man still had the gun pointed at me, but his energy was not the same. The heat and rage were not as pronounced.

"You don't know me. You see me in a suit and tie, and you saw a successful businessman. You don't know my past or what I've done." Everything I said before this was mostly for my safety. I didn't see a man trying to rob me or that my life was in danger anymore. Now I saw a lost young man.

The young man didn't yell this time, and all of the anger was gone. "My daughter is sick. I need money. I didn't want to rob you. I saw you walking."

"My only child passed," I told him. "If there was anything I could have done to help her, I can't say what I would have done." I started taking off my watch.

"What are you doing?" The young man raised his voice, but he wasn't yelling. This was more like passion and confusion than anger.

I told him I only had a few hundred dollars on me, but that my watch was worth much, much more.

"I can't take anything from you!" Tears started coming from the young man's eyes. He reached his hand out to help me up. Once I was on my feet, he said, "I'm sorry. I'm sorry." He saw the mud all over my clothes and noticed that my suit was ruined.

"It's just clothes," I said to make him feel better.

He began to explain his situation. He had just gotten out of prison. I told him I served time as well, but I was blessed with a second chance. While he was getting out, his mother was going in. Not only did he have a sick child to think about but he also had siblings who needed a place to live. He didn't have a stable place for himself yet. I told him I had been homeless as well, and as a teenager. But again, I was blessed and my life was completely different now.

I asked if I could pray for him. We prayed together, as Christian and Muslim brothers. After we finished praying, I asked his name so I could properly address him, and we talked for the next thirty minutes. I gave him my number, but he did not have a phone yet. He gave me a friend's number.

I got to work that same night! I called dozens of people I knew until I found someone who was willing to hire him, as a favor to me. The next day, I worked with the same legislators from the event to secure housing for his family.

I gave him hope and my friendship. Once I was able to see what was causing the young man to do the things he did, everything shifted. I did not see a dangerous person with a gun. I saw a young man who was just as nervous as me. I saw a person who was acting out of hopelessness.

There is always a reason. People have a reason for doing everything they do and usually have a more understandable reason than you would have thought.

In the middle of an extremely dangerous situation, my focus was on what caused us to arrive at this point. What was the root cause that sparked the flame that was burning? Once I understood that, I could get us both back to a safe place, without anyone getting hurt. It was not enough to just make sure I didn't get hurt. I could also make sure no one else was placed in the same position by truly destroying the bridge that led the young man to the dark space he was in.

Even though I could have lost my life, I had to take into consideration the entire life of the young man. He did not come into the world as a baby who wanted to hurt people once he finally became an adult. At one point, he had dreams, and they were positive. Over the course of his life, life happened. Something affected him. The negative action I was dealing with was motivated by something. Behind whatever that thing is, there is still that good person. His dreams still existed.

As youth change agents, it is our jobs to identify the barriers that are keeping our youth from being hopeful about their lives. Once we understand what is motiving these negative behaviors, we can restore their hope and then help them gain the tools needed to succeed, without resorting to criminality or other self-destructive actions. This is what I will discuss.

KEY FIRST STEP

Look at the things the youth tells you from their perspective, not yours. Your goal is to understand why they think the way they do. Ask questions that give him or her the chance to explain why they feel, think, and act the way they do. If they told you they did something, ask why they did that, follow up by asking how the experience made them feel, and then ask if they would do the same thing the same way now—and allow them to fully explain.

Why Youth Change Agents Are So Critical

A mentor is someone who allows you
to see the hope inside yourself.

—Oprah Winfrey

Before discussing how to be an effective youth change agent, let's address:

- Why youth change agents are so critical
- What a youth change agent is changing
- Why high-risk youth deserve a change agent
- What you are committing to when you agree to become a change agent

Why Change Agents Are So Critical

A change agent may be the difference between life and death for a youth. That child may not have another positive figure in their life. Your presence and the impact you make could easily be the factor that changes their life. The lessons you teach them can alter their entire future.

If all a person has access to are toxic influences, what reason do they have to be hopeful about life? How exactly would they become a positive person? If a child grows up in a dark and negative environment, how would they know things can be better? If someone sees just about everyone around them using crime as a way to resolve problems, how would they know what is wrong? If a child sees their own parents abuse substances or are involved in gangs, what's keeping them from doing the same?

If everyone in a child's life is consistently stressed and usually seems unhappy because they struggle to provide the basic things they need, live in horrible and dangerous conditions, or are barely able to keep a roof over their head from month to month, they can easily believe struggling is just a part of life for working-class adults and people who make their money legally. This could lead to misconceptions in the mind of a child. For example, he or she may see little value in school. Why earn an education if you are going to struggle anyway? Remember, they haven't witnessed how earning an education improved or changed anyone's life. They could become comfortable with living in poverty because they think it's the only option they have, since everyone around them is in poverty. They could start committing crimes to make extra money because they believe that's the only way they can make enough money to change their situation.

This can be true in many different ways and areas of life. If a child grows up hearing their parents yelling every time they have a disagreement or problem, why wouldn't they believe it is normal for people in a relationship to yell when there is a disagreement? If a parent threatens to hit them as a part of disciplining them, they may not take a disciplinarian seriously, unless they threaten to use physical force. Pretty much all their life, that child experiences yelling and physical force as a sign that things were becoming more serious. How does the child know things are serious without the identifying factors they are taught and are accustomed to?

What if a child grows up in a heavily gang-influenced community? By the time the child reaches middle school, most of their peers may already be in gangs or developing some type of connection with them. What if the gangs are in the child's home because their parents or older siblings are connected to gangs? They may look at the people in a gang as uncles or like a big sibling because they are around so much and not see them as bad influences.

The same child may see people go to college, but they see far more people go to prison or killed than make it to college. They also most likely live in communities with mostly fatherless homes or lack access to two-parent homes. They may also witness their own parents abusing substances in their own home daily or they can be exposed to the same behavior from other adults in their community daily. It may be normal for the people around them to lie, curse, litter, and overlook the needs of others because they are already overwhelmed and stressed from their own challenges. Asking youth to be better than the adults around them is a hard request, especially when they have no access to anyone to teach them how to do so.

What Is a Change Agent Changing?

A youth change agent is the person who comes into a youth's life and seeks to change what they believe. For many youth, there may only be one person who comes into their life to do this, so the role that person plays is critical to their survival and development. A change agent changes what the youth sees as possible. A change agent also changes what seems normal, what's acceptable, and what's not. A change agent adjusts what seems negative and what type of energy youth want around them or want to produce.

In short, a change agent introduces a new way of thinking. By introducing new elements, a change agent challenges the old things in a youth's life. A person cannot decide if something is right or wrong if they never had choices or weren't aware that they did. If you are only provided one choice, you are going to take what's offered. Chicken will be your favorite food if you only have chicken restaurants in your community and you are forced to eat chicken daily because that is all you have access to. Regardless if the food is unhealthy or hurts your family to feed it to them, if you always thought there was only one way to do something, that's how you are going to do it.

Just showing up is powerful and impactful. When a change agent allows a youth access to their world, they are already changing that youth's perspective on life because they are proving that something different exists and is possible. Change agents can introduce a new way of thinking and being just by being themselves. When a change agent brings a child into their environment, they are widening the youth's exposure. By being a positive person in their life, change agents also bring a new perspective on how people can be in another person's life.

Please know: everything about a change agent and what they do is making an impression. For this reason, it is important that change agents are aware and very intentional in the way they treat the youth they work with. They should be a good visual example—and consistent. It's like the saying, "a child does what they see you do, not what they hear you say." Truthfully, they are doing both. Children are observing everything they can visually see and whatever they hear. Even if a change agent doesn't mean for them to hear or see something, if they do, it's downloaded and processed. They may not know what to do with the information yet, but they have it for life.

Why Higher-Risk Youth Deserve Change Agents

A higher-risk youth is someone whose social determinants, behavior, and/or actions increase their odds of negative things happening in their life or reduce their odds of success. These social determinants can include their home situation, lifestyle, or living conditions. It could also be the community they live in, the things they are exposed to, or what they lack exposure to. They may live in a high-crime community, around violence, or have high level of exposure to illegal drugs. They may attend schools with limited resources. It could also be their own behavior that increases their risks—they could be making poor decisions that increase their level of risks. All youth face the risks of being in the wrong place at the wrong time, involving themselves with the wrong peers, and making poor decisions, but these are just a few factors that place a youth in a higher risk category.

Many youth who grow up in higher-risk conditions do not have access to several of the opportunities that seem normal for many other people. The youth may have grown up without a stable home or family or nurturing environment, making it extremely difficult to develop properly. They could have been forced to deal with adult issues and responsibilities as a child, which stopped them from being able to focus on things other children their age did that helped them develop thoroughly and properly. Their struggles could have been so extreme they felt pushed to make poor decisions just to survive.

Far too often, a higher-risk youth's life is determined for them or they may have to work much harder to change the direction of their future. They are at a disadvantage because of someone else's limitations, poor decisions, mistakes, actions, and/or bad luck. Their parents may not have prepared properly to be a parent, they could have been a child themselves when they had their first child, or they could have suffered devastating events that pulled them backward. Regardless of what caused their situation, a child is growing up with a harder life, fewer resources, negative exposure, limited opportunity, or in a very dangerous environment—and it is happening because of things they had absolutely no control over. Here are some common circumstances that put a child at higher risk.

Substance Abuse, Addiction, and Disability

If a parent has a substance abuse addiction that prevents them from properly parenting their child and no one else is there, how do you think that affects the child? How many things does a parent typically teach their child that help the child develop prior to starting school? In a good household, what type of experiences help nurture a child in a healthy way? Many things other people may see as normal, a child in a home with a parent with these struggles may never experience. Hearing someone say they love them, seeing their parent set a goal then work to reach it, or simply seeing their family celebrate life together—those all may be unheard of for them. The things they may see daily could be the complete opposite. Unbelievable experiences for the average person and unspeakable circumstances could easily be a part of their everyday life. A child growing up in a home with a parent with severe substance abuse issues may easily be raising themself—due to their parent's inability to perform the day-to-day duties of a parent. Substance abuse is just one of the many roads that could leave a child in this position. The parent could have a gambling problem, anger issues, be in the club or streets more than they are home, or like I mentioned earlier, they may be a child trying to raise a child. Then there are also parents with other physical and mental health challenges. No matter how much they want or try, they just are not capable of properly caring for someone else.

Poverty and Parent Absenteeism

What if the parent is struggling to provide for their child or children to the point where they are barely and rarely present? Let's say the parent is working a job that pays them $10 per hour and it costs $2,000 or more a month just to provide a place to live and necessities for the family. That parent may have to work two jobs because one doesn't produce enough. Then what if that parent has to take public transportation to get to work? Their commute could easily be three to four hours each day to get back and forth to work. They may work six hours at one job and seven at another. That's sixteen or seventeen hours a day they spend outside their home— just to make sure their child has a place to call home.

Let's say that the parent also sleeps five hours a day; twenty-two hours out of their day is already accounted for. When do they have time to do the basic things a parent should do with their child? Not to mention, this parent is most likely under an overwhelming amount of pressure; they are trying to keep everything together, with very few resources. They are trying to make sure their child *survives* childhood, so they cannot focus on creating *the ideal* childhood.

What if this is the way the parent grew up? They could see life as this hard thing that you do whatever you have to just to keep your head above water because that's the way it's been for them all their life. They may not be able to help their child see the world as a place with limitless opportunities because the world never offered that to them. They may not have left the area they live in to let their child or children know how life feels for people who live less than twenty miles away.

Community and Education

The child may also live in a very unsafe and/or unhealthy community: If many of the families in their neighborhood face similar challenges, the community can easily be overwhelmed with violence and crime. This is the result of people attempting to survive with very little access to resources, so they turn to crime, which makes the community even more violent.

In the case of education, a child may go to a school that struggles to provide the same level of access to services and support as a school a few miles away. If the funds raised through property tax create a large part of the budget for the school, a lower-income community will struggle to support its local schools the same way because the homes are a lower value and do not raise nearly the same taxes. This alone means the schools will have fewer resources and staff. The school is attempting to fulfill additional needs other districts' students do not face and has to ask much more out of teachers they have and pay them a fraction of the salary other schools offer. Add to that, the schools do not have the same level of family and community support because the parents are working so many more hours due to making a fraction of what parents across town are paid. The community simply cannot offer the resources because they don't have them to offer. This means you have underpaid and overwhelmed staff attempting to be secondary parents, mentors, big brothers and sisters, aunts and uncles, coaches, role models, and tutors because their students lack so many resources within their home, inside their community, plus they may face systematic discrimination and disadvantages other children will never know exist.

These are just a few situations. No matter the situation, the result is usually the same: a child who grows up in less-than-ideal conditions, lacks exposure, witnesses things no child should have to see, is not nurtured properly, develops a less positive view of the world, and does not have anyone there to walk them through life step by step. Things that other children see as normal—talking to their parents about their day, family dinners, or taking a summer vacation—they may never experience.

Giving Youth a Fair First Chance

When you put all of this together, you have a child who never really had a fair chance. They were born into a rough situation. They did not do anything to create any of these conditions. They did not pick their challenges or what influenced them. Despite all of this, every one of these factors completely altered their upbringing. Our upbringings prepare each of us for the life we will live as adults.

Everyone deserves a chance to take control of their destiny. To determine what type of life they will create for themself. To control how they will feel about their life. To put in the work to earn the life they want. To write their own story, despite their social determinants.

Every day of our childhood can be looked at as a block we are given. These blocks are used to pave the road we travel down to the world as an adult. They create the foundation we build our adult life on. Let's imagine that we get more blocks with every positive experience, when we are taught new things, or from positive exposure. If a child lacks these opportunities, they will have very few blocks. As a result, their road will never take them very far from what they come from or give them the chance to build a strong foundation for a strong and bright future.

When a change agent enters their life, the child gains new building blocks. Making time to talk, three new blocks. When a change agent gives them a reason to challenge what they had been told was a limit or they believed was the only way something could be, ten new blocks. When a change agent lets them see how people live in places they never had access to or did not know existed, thirty more blocks. As a change agent allows a youth to see that while they are different, they have more similarities than it may seem, one hundred more blocks. When a change agent explains how they became the person they are today, despite their own challenges, one thousand blocks!

When a change agent gives a child a reason to have hope, they give them the ability to build an unlimited number of blocks for themself!

What You Are Committing to as a Change Agent

As a change agent, the first person you actually make a commitment to is you. Change agents cannot pour from an empty cup. It is critical to be the best version of yourself possible. Change agents must be aware of their own emotions and care about them. Give yourself what you need and be good to you.

Everything a change agent does is setting an example. What a change agent doesn't do is also an example; if a change agent has bad habits that put them in danger, the change agent needs to address that. Change agents should be aware and accountable—not perfect, but a work in progress. A change agent needs to have a life plan, with goals, and all the things they want for the young person they are working with—how can a change agent inspire a youth to have hope in their life if the change agent is not hopeful about their own future?

Change agents also need to set boundaries. You need to know what you will and won't do with or for the youth you're working with. What is the line you won't cross and why? What do you feel comfortable talking about and what's outside of your comfort zone? Who is the ideal youth for them to be paired with based on age, gender, background, and so on? If a change agent is willing to work with any child, regardless of who they are and their background, that is great. The same thorough process still needs to be followed every time. The change agent should be as detailed as possible and write out a full list describing who they can work with and best connect with and then explain why. It is essential to be thorough: any details overlooked or left out could negatively affect a youth's life later.

Journaling is important. One of the best exercises a change agent can ask a youth to do is to keep a journal and write daily for at least fifteen minutes; however, a change agent should never ask a youth to do something they have not done or would not do. So, they should start a journal prior to working with anyone. Part of the journaling process should include taking a personal inventory of their daily journey as a change agent. If you already journal, great. Just add this part.

I honestly believe once a change agent gets themself in a great space intentionally, they've done the most difficult part. Now they are just continuing the same level of care they put into themself and in their life. Again, the things they want for themself, they should want for the youth they work with. Now that you have yourself covered and taken care of, we can address your commitment to the youth you pledged to be a change agent for.

Would you want someone to be in and out of your life? Of course not. Be consistent. Once a change agent comes into a youth's life, they matter to that youth, so being dependable matters. Many high-risk youth have already experienced more than enough people coming and going. Also, a change agent must make sure to hear the youth they work with and value them the same way they value themself. Take the time to learn who a youth wants to be, then assist them and help them work toward their goals as a team.

An amazing change agent honors the commitment of caring about the youth in their life the same way they care about themself, sees the youth as a person with their own hopes and dreams, and respects both of their boundaries!

KEY FIRST STEP

Take an honest assessment of your whys. Why are you becoming a change agent? Why is this important to you? Why do you believe higher-risk youth deserve and need a change agent?

Then follow the same process with your whats. What do you believe it means to be to be a change agent, and are you up to that? What are you hoping to accomplish by becoming a change agent? What would you like to see changed in the life of the youth you work with? What do you want to see the outcome in a youth's life be as a result of what you change together? What are you willing to sacrifice and invest to make those things happen?

Gain Trust

Trust is delicate and fragile to
gain, with sincerity it leads to the
golden foundation for success.

—Akinwumi Jarule

Most likely, a change agent has no idea what the child or young adult they are attempting to work with has been through. Even the most qualified change agent cannot look at a child and assume they are like the children they are used to. Everyone has scars, and we often hold on to the memories of how we got each scar.

The person a change agent works with may have grown up in a household where they were constantly letdown. They could have been taught to not trust or depend on anyone but themself. They may have been yelled at and frightened by their parents every time they did something that upset them. They may have been verbally or physically abused. An adult may have touched them in a way no child should be touched. They could have witnessed things no child should have to see. They could have been promised things over and over that never came. Over the years, the child could have been forced to grow up quicker than they should have.

Children in single-parent homes are often forced to grow up faster than children with both parents, depending on the support system the single parent has and the circumstances they live in. A child with only one parent may have to do things the average child their age couldn't imagine because the parent has to work more hours to provide just the basics or is absent for other reasons. As a result, the parent spends more time away from the home. Things one child has their parents there to do, another child may have to do for themself. If the child has smaller siblings or family members with special needs, they may also be a caregiver.

A four-year-old who was raised in a community that has an extremely high crime rate may have seen things the change agent working with them hasn't even seen as an adult. For example, what if the child lives in a home where the adults are the criminals? Just think about what they could see every single day! That four-year-old could have watched people lie quicker and more often than they tell the truth, use each other to get what they want, or even regularly hurt people.

These are just a few circumstances youth change agents may see. Regardless of the difficult circumstances a high-risk youth may come from, one aspect is likely true for all: the environment they're used to might have taught them the only person they can trust is themself.

The Impact of Negative Exposure

I use age four for a specific reason. When I sold drugs, it was common for parents to have children in the home when they bought drugs. Some people were raised around drugs themselves, and drugs just became a common part of life. Since no one kept drugs away from them, they didn't see why they needed to keep them away from their children.

However, I had a custom. Before I came inside anyone's house, I'd ask them to put their children in another room. I didn't bring drugs around children.

One day, I went to a guy's house to sell him a few thousand dollars' worth of crack. At the time, I had been selling drugs for a while, so I only sold drugs to other drug dealers. Because we spent so much time around each other, I knew all of their kids and their families. The guy I was visiting sold drugs mostly at night, and he watched his young son all day until his older son got home from school.

While we were weighing up what he was buying from me, his four-year-old son ran into the room. I didn't have time to put the drugs away or block him from seeing them. Just by looking at the drugs on the table, his son guessed the amount of drugs his father was buying because the little boy had been around drugs and criminal activity so much. He hadn't even started school yet, but he knew how to measure crack by eyesight and then convert grams to ounces—and he knew the value of each unit.

Another child may have lived in a violent house or community. After seeing multiple people get hurt, they may see the world as a dangerous and violent place; they may have even been hurt themself, which could easily further damage their trust. For their own safety, they could have learned not to trust the world or to keep people at a certain distance. They could be physically protecting themself, or it could be their mental well-being they're guarding. Children who live rougher lives can put up walls to protect them from disappointment.

Let's face it: The children a change agent is working with may have never had a person in their life that had their best interest in mind, or it may be so uncommon, that they don't believe that a person could truly care about them that way. A change agent may have the best intentions, but in the beginning of the relationship with the child, the change agent is the only person who knows that. In the child's mind, they may believe everyone has some alternative motive. The child could push a change agent away because it's easier to push them away than to wait until they leave because person after person who came into their life may have left just as quickly as they came. They could be tired of people leaving, without a warning, right when they think someone finally cares.

Building Trust through Service

Several years ago, I received a call from a teacher I regularly worked with. In schools, I'm seen as the go-to person for male students from inner-city communities who are having serious behavior issues. Because of my ability to connect with students who are starting to engage in illegal activities, teachers or school staff will call me directly when they are worried about one of their students.

The teacher called because a student she was pretty hands-on with just disappeared and she was worried about what he was doing since he wasn't coming to school. I talked to the young man she was worried about over the phone. She had good reason to worry: he had joined a gang. He wasn't going to school because he was spending time with the gang members. They were working on building an unbreakable bond with him.

After a few conversations, he and I went to lunch to connect in person. My goal was to gain his trust, so I asked a few questions as an icebreaker. I didn't ask questions because I was interested in the answers he gave me—I wanted to learn what type of attention and energy made him feel valued. The more I let him talk freely, I could tell he appreciated just being heard. I only asked questions when he slowed down so he would keep talking and I could show him I was still listening. The more I listened, the more he talked.

After our third time meeting for lunch, something different happened. The young man stopped talking and became very emotional. He told me no one had ever shown up so much for him or made him feel like they genuinely cared before. All I did up to that point was be there when he needed someone and listen.

From that day forward, he asked my opinion on every major issue in his life without me ever requesting that he take my advice, all because I gained his trust thoroughly by showing up, which let him know how much he meant to me. Because the young man gave me his trust, it opened a completely new door in our relationship. Now I could talk with him, instead of just listening to him.

Now I could introduce new ideas. I started to change the type of conversations we had: I started conversations that made him think. Every time I allowed him to vent, I learned critical things. I knew what his highest risks were because he told me. I also knew his dreams and goals. I was able to understand what he was doing that could hurt him. I also knew his organic motivators and saw what would naturally keep him focused on making positive changes when no one was there to support him because he allowed me to see what he really wanted out of life.

With greater insight, I was ready to be his mentor. When I introduced aspects of his life that he needed to change, he trusted my opinion because he trusted me. When I introduced him to new people who could give him exposure to different areas of life, he was open to meeting them because I had never let him down before, and everything I introduced was now an extension of me. So, if he trusted me, then he could trust them enough to see how they could be helpful. If something didn't work or became too much, he wasn't worried because he knew he wasn't in this alone.

Since I was constantly there before when he needed me, he knew I would be there again. The relationship we built was the foundation for everything that came later. Not only did he trust me but he also trusted the process. Trusting me taught him it was okay to trust that good things could happen. He also learned to trust himself. Each time something good happened, he dove more into trusting that his future could be better than his past.

Without building trust first, he probably would have never allowed me to invest in his life.

The Power of Trust

Change agents don't need to have all the answers or have access to every social work tool, but once a change agent has trust, the change agent and the child can work together as a team and figure it out as they go. Each positive thing a change agent introduces eliminates the need for something negative that was in that youth's life, or it takes up space so they don't have room for what they were doing before.

For example, a child may start selling drugs so they can feed themself. For another, it may seem like the only option is to join the gang so they can have access to drugs and have permission to sell them in their neighborhood.

A change agent's presence in their life proves that it's possible to survive without taking that type of risk or hurting others. Now they see other options exist. Since the child they're working with trusts them, they're going to trust what they expose them to.

The same child and a change agent can work together to find another way to earn money—legally. Their change agent helped them gain new skills and exposure by getting them a job and encouraging them to work. Because they now have a job, they do not have to be around the gang they were willing to join. Because they have a job and are busy working, they do not have time to be in the streets. They can't be around bad influences all day if they must go to work daily. Also, now they gain exposure because they leave their environment to go into a work environment. They adjust to being in a workplace setting, show up to the same place on time daily, work as a team with others, fulfill a position, finish things they start, and participate in several other positive experiences. They also meet people they may have never been around or connected to.

Giving the young person something positive to do and be a part of creates a completely new mindset. The change agent didn't know exactly what to do in the beginning, but they both figured it out together—because they trusted each other.

KEY FIRST STEP

Ask the youth about his or her upbringing and personal interests and then listen intently. Based on what you hear, list five ways you believe you can gain their trust.

Seeing the Youth in Front of You

The key to being a good mentor is to help
people become more of who they already
are—not to make them more like you.

—*Suze Orman*

It is easy to think we know a person. Sometimes, after just
a glimpse, we put them into a box. We may only know a
small part of their story, yet we judge them on the things
we believe to be true.

A youth's life may remind us of our own. We may connect with them because of our similarities. We may come
from a similar background. Before we even know who the

youth is, we may feel connected to them. We might live in the same city or even the same neighborhood. We may face the same types of challenges. A youth may remind us of someone—maybe a person who was close to us. That person could be us, at a different point in our life. Whatever the connection is, a simple connection can build a bond. That connection may cause us to care about them.

No change agent wants to push a child away. However, the same quick judgment that motivates us to help one child could cause us to turn our back on another one. This may be the first experience youth have had in this space and simply do not know how to receive a person. Before we give them a chance, we may have already made a decision about them. This could be based on the actions of someone in our past. We could turn our back on a child whose entire life could change if they had one change agent to show up and invest in them. We may have seen people like them before. Things we've heard other people say or how other people we've watched behave could influence us, perhaps in real life, music, or television shows. All this could happen subconsciously.

This is why it is so important that we are aware of the things that motivate and trigger us. We all have them. If a change agent does not understand how dangerous this is, they can easily unfairly judge youth. As a result, we can pick and choose who we help or care about. We could also unfairly punish youth who have not done anything to deserve such treatment. Change agents can become biased without being aware of it. A change agent who does this will most likely fail with the youth they try to support.

See the Youth in Front of You

Each child is unique. The child in front of a change agent may remind them of themself. They may be unbelievably similar to someone the change agent grew up with. The change agent may have raised children who a youth reminds them of. Maybe they worked with or around children longer than the child they're about to work with has been alive.

The child in front of that change agent is not them. They also are not their child. They are not one of the thousands of students who came through a change agent's classroom. They are not one of the kids a change agent coached or mentored before. The youth in front of a change agent is their own person. They have their own past, as well as their own dreams. All of their experiences have worked together to mold them in a very unique way.

How can we effectively help a person who we don't truly understand? How can a change agent understand a person who they haven't taken the time to know? If a change agent is giving someone something that does not fit them, what's the odds they will want it? How can a change agent give someone what they need or want, if they don't know the child in front of them?

The only way a change agent can get to know the youth they're working with is by putting the time in to know them. Change agents have to allow youth to show who they are. There is no quick way to cheat the process. Assessments and personality tests can tell a change agent about someone and give insight, but they are only tools that help develop the relationship. The best assessment still won't and can't build a relationship for a change agent—you have to do that for yourself.

One teenager I worked with started a fire inside his school. The fire began in the bathroom. He set paper inside the trash can on fire, then threw the trash can in the hallway. You would have thought this kid would have run, but he didn't. He didn't care if he was caught. He didn't care if he was hurt. He didn't care if he was killed. He didn't care about anything, and it seemed like he didn't care about anyone.

Fortunately, the fire didn't spread because the emergency sprinkler system triggered and extinguished the flames. A large part of the school filled with thick smoke. But the fire could have burned down the entire school. If the fire had continued to burn, students and teachers might have been hurt, or worse.

Police were called and the student was handcuffed and detained. The administration had to make a decision. Students do reckless things. Some of the things they do are dangerous, but can be handled in school, while others reach another level.

Do you arrest the student and charge them with arson, expel them, suspend them, or treat this is as simply a dangerous mistake that went further than expected? It was a hard decision to make. No one who dedicates their life to saving youth wants to be the person who puts them in a position that is going to derail them. Once a child enters the criminal justice system, we all know what that means for them. He wouldn't have the opportunity to go to another school and likely would be incarcerated, possibly for a lengthy amount of time.

The administration looked at the video cameras and couldn't see what happened in the bathroom. But what the cameras did show was a young man with seemingly no regard for human life. A young man who had hate in him. A young man who could not control his anger. Someone who did not see how his actions impacted everyone around him.

Nevertheless, every student was like family to this particular administration, so they cared about the young man, despite his actions. The school served students from a low-income and rough community. Most of the students lived in poverty or close to it. When teachers and administrators at the school saw students struggling, they stepped in where they could to help, like providing students with fresh clothes and even getting diapers for some of the students' younger siblings or children. School was more than a place to be educated; it was a community center and a second home.

Administrators sought my advice about what they should do with the student. When I walked into the school's office that day, the student was about to be arrested and expelled. Because our agency creates and provides behavioral programs for several schools, we have earned enough respect to have a seat at the table during critical times. When schools have major behavioral issues, they allow us to consult and help determine what actions need to be taken.

What I saw was behavior that did not match the personality of the student. He had never done anything like this before. When I got a chance to talk to him, I didn't ask him questions about the fire but rather, simply another question: How he was doing? When I did, he broke down into tears and opened up. His brother had been shot a few days earlier. His cousin was shot—and killed—the day before that. Both were shot in his neighborhood. His cousin was shot right in front of him in their driveway. Yet, the young man came to school shortly after witnessing that.

When he revealed that information, the room was silent. For the first time, everyone *saw him*, completely. They saw this young man who was going through more than anyone could imagine. It wasn't about a fire now. It was about a person who was trying to survive. It was clear he was going through overwhelming grief and trauma.

So, what happened to the student who set the fire? Instead of expelling him, we discussed what could we do to keep him safe. We asked, "How do we help him heal?" The handcuffs came off, and a plan was developed.

Every morning, he got to school before the other students to help staff with random tasks and he was taught accountability. He stayed after school every day for months to clean up the damages he caused and then assist as replacements were made.

We created a plan that kept him safe. He was barely at home or in the community. We weren't able to change his environment, but we kept him out of it until it became safe. As a result, he is a college graduate now, instead of a convicted felon.

KEY FIRST STEP

Keep an open mind about the youth you are meeting. Remember every youth is their own person, with their own thoughts, experiences, and personality. At this stage, ask personal questions related to things you've already discussed together that assist you with getting to know the person you're working with and keeping the conversation going.

Being True to You

Every great achiever is inspired
by a great mentor.
—*Lailah Gifty Akita*

Not to dissuade you in any way from becoming a youth change agent, but make sure you're up to the task. Understand how serious your role will be in a young person's life. The direction you give could affect that person for the rest of their life. Take a moment to *be true to yourself* and make sure you really want to be a change agent in a young person's life.

According to the organization Youth Mentor, "Students who meet regularly with their mentors are 52 percent less likely than their peers to skip a day of school and 37 percent less likely to skip a class. Youth who meet regularly with their mentors are 46 percent less likely than their peers to start using illegal drugs and 27 percent less likely to start drinking. Sixty-seven percent of at-risk young adults who had a mentor aspire to enroll in and graduate from college versus half of at-risk young adults who had no mentor." Youth Mentor also reported that mentors reduce depression symptoms and increase social acceptance, academic attitudes, and grades.

While mentoring can be a powerful tool, it could also be a harmful weapon. For example, according to Jean E. Rhodes and her colleagues in *Urban Girls Revisited: Building Strengths*, "growing evidence suggests that a close and enduring connection must form in order for youth to benefit from a mentoring relationship. Relationships that are less close tend to have little effect, and those of short duration can actually make matters worse for some youth." The difference depends on how well it is done and how dedicated the mentor is.

You are opening your life up. You are investing in a person. You are doing all of this out of the kindness of your heart. You are not asking for anything in return. You have to be emotionally invested and available. Life can already be demanding, but you are adding the weight of another person to your life. You give your time to learn how to effectively reach and teach a person, even though you may never be compensated for the work you do. You may even be taking time away from your own family to give to another youth.

Caring about someone, taking an interest in their future, and being there for them are remarkable investments to make into another person's life and selfless endeavors, but difficult, especially over the long term. Are you willing to be well trained, available, focused, and determined? Why do you want to help this person? Are you willing to give something you will never be able to replace or recover—your time? Why will you put in time and work to care for a young person you may not even know?

Fighting for a Chance to Help

Anyone should appreciate a person caring about them and wanting to help. Yet, sometimes mentors feel they have to beg youth to let them care and help them. Sometimes, mentors show up for a youth and they don't want their help. If someone makes a choice, we should respect their decision, shouldn't we?

Normally I would agree, but not this time. We have no idea what the youth who change agents are working with or hope to work with has been through. It is normal for youth who come from troubled backgrounds to be very slow to trust. A youth may have been taken advantage of. They may have watched other people get hurt by people they trusted. They may have been abandoned or mistreated by the people they thought should have been there to help, and as a result, they learned that it is safer to keep people at a distance because they cannot be disappointed by someone they never expect anything from or hurt by someone they do not allow to get close.

A mother reached out and asked if I could work with her son who had been arrested for possession of illegal drugs. Like any mother, she was worried and afraid. This was her baby boy. She made her son the number one priority in her life from the day he was born. Whatever her son needed, she found a way to make it happen. No matter what it took, no matter how afraid she was, or how big the challenge was, she was up to the challenge for her son, and this was no different—this strong woman refused to let her son get pulled into the streets, die as the result of a bad drug deal, or end up in prison.

From our very first conversation, both the mother and son impressed me. He was just as passionate and determined as his mother. You could tell watching his mother be so relentless for her family influenced him as a child. Her son's passion was motivated by his desire to be something. Like most children, he wanted to make his mother proud. Like most sons, he wanted to provide. He wanted to give his mother the life she deserved. Watching how hard his hero worked to build a home and keep him safe birthed an unstoppable urge inside of him.

This is not the story of a child who turned to drugs to create a way out of the hood. This young man did not turn to crime at all. He turned to a mentor. After deciding he wanted to go into a specific profession, he searched until he found a mentor in that industry. This way, before investing money and time he didn't have to waste, he could make sure this was what he wanted to do with his future. This was the only future he had, and there was a family dependent on this working.

However, the young man's biggest mistake was being connected with the wrong mentor. Instead of learning how to enter his profession, his so-called mentor took him in an entirely different direction. In the beginning, the mentor shared his story and showed him what it took to open doors. This is what any good mentor-mentee relationship would look like. What happened next was anything but normal. His mentor gave him drugs and asked him to sell them for him.

As soon as the mentor saw trust developing, he manipulated it. The relationship continued for a while. The more drugs the mentee sold, the more time he earned to be educated and gain access to exposure. When he was finally arrested, everything changed.

The person he trusted stopped answering his calls then eventually changed his number and blocked his mentee on all of his social media accounts. The man he thought was going to change his life did exactly what he said he would, just not in the way anyone thought. He helped his mentee become a convicted felon and then abandoned him. Overnight, the mentee went from being praised to finding out he was being preyed on.

The Impact of a Mentor

This is not the type of mentor you will be. I want to emphasize the impact you can have on a person's life though. Because you're taking the time to read this book, I believe you have good intentions. I urge you to be vested in what you're doing and always remember why you wanted to be a mentor, which will keep you from ever being pulled in the wrong direction and make earning your mentee's trust and then handling it with care easier.

After someone has been hurt by a person they trusted, it becomes difficult to believe in anyone else. It takes courage to trust, and sometimes, you have to help someone build that trust back up. This is why we have to be willing to do so much work before the real work begins. The youth who needs you the most may be the most difficult to reach. What will happen to them if you walk away?

I was able to earn the young man's trust, which was not easy. After his trust in the previous mentor had been broken, he was not quick to place himself in the same position. I had to show up and let him see I cared before I could expect anything at all in return. Due to our connection, he used the tools I helped him learn and created a new plan to reach his goals. His legal issues and everything that had happened became a motivator. We introduced him to the right people this time. He not only regained control over his life, but he is now also much further along than he anticipated and understands why succeeding the right way is critical. What would have happened if I had given up before I knew his situation? Because he seemed difficult and did not appreciate the investment I wanted to make into his life?

Some youth have experienced abandonment. They believed that someone would be there and that person disappeared. This may have been a parent who walked away or who was absent the child's entire life. They may have lost people to sudden and unexpected death. People they loved may have been murdered, and it felt like they just disappeared because there was never any closure.

You may have to help a youth get over their past before you can start working on their present or toward their future. But if you're sincere, and patient, you can make a difference—in a good way.

KEY FIRST STEP

Take time to write a letter to yourself. In this letter, explain why you want to invest in the life of youth. Be as detailed as possible.

Making a Connection

Every child deserves a champion—
an adult who will never give up on
them, who understands the power of
connection, and insists that they become
the best that they can possibly be.

—Rita F. Pierson

The first family I ever worked with was an entire family unit. This was before I founded my agency or started my journey in social work. I met the mother because she was selling her car. I saw it in a parking lot with a for sale sign. The make of the car was one I had been looking for, so I decided to pull over and inquire.

When I met the mother, she opened up about her reason for selling the car. She was behind on the rent, so she was desperate. She said it was better to lose their car than their home. The car appeared to be in good condition, but it wasn't. I knew she was going to struggle trying to sell it. I happened to have the money she was asking for the car on me at the time, so I decided to buy it.

But instead of taking the car, I let her keep it. I told her she could continue to drive the car and I would come get it when I was ready. The young lady was a proud woman. She did not want a handout. Just to get her to take the money, I had to convince her that she was doing me a favor. I lied and told her that I didn't have a place to keep the car, that it might get towed if I left it parked.

I knew money for the car would help her for the month, but what about next month, then the month after that? How would she get back and forth to work? She had children. How would not having a car impact the quality of life for the children? I didn't need the car and the money I gave her did not affect me, so it was better to just help her.

As a result of that day, I ended up developing a relationship with her entire family. She gleaned that I worked with youth. She reached out one day and asked if I could talk with her oldest son, who had just returned home after serving a short prison sentence. Like any mother, she was worried about her son, but he was not her biggest concern. She feared the impact his actions would have on her other sons: a younger teenage son and an even younger son. Both of them looked up to the older brother. Whatever he did, they wanted to do.

I built a relationship with the oldest son. The same way the younger brothers looked at him, he started to look at me. As a result of the connection we built, I was able to shift his view on life. I let him see how being in the streets had impacted me. We were able to understand each other because I had been where he was. He thought hustling would be his way out. I used to think that. Things he was doing to make a name for himself, I had done.

I was able to connect with him. Not only did I understand the mindset that motivated his actions, but I also saw him as a person. I had been in a similar place as him, but I knew I wasn't him and he wasn't me. I used my past to allow me to care about his situation, but I listened to the things he told me to understand his situation. I let him tell me who he was and why he did the things he did. I was transparent with him—no one else had done that. I shared my past and told him anything he asked. I knew I couldn't expect him to be honest or open with me if I wasn't all of those things with him first.

I knew I had to emotionally connect with him as a person, but I also knew I had to help him survive as well. I found him a job. It wasn't much, but it was enough to keep him out the streets. He made enough money to take care of himself and enjoy being a teenager. The job exposed him to a different culture. He met guys his own age who weren't in the streets but were still cool. The more he worked, the more I could see the desire to be in the streets leave. He saw he was able to become the person he wanted to be without having to turn to the streets.

He and his siblings were extremely close. His changes made it a lot easier to help his siblings make positive changes. Just like his mother thought: Wherever he went, his little brothers followed. And their little sister adored all of them because they were her world.

Their mother worked around the clock to take care of them and provide the best quality of life possible. However, the children were left alone far more often than their mother liked. But since the children were all they had and were always together, they were unbelievably attached to each other. I was able to get the younger brothers more attached to their schooling. I signed them up for sports and other activities. After I developed a personal connection with them, I learned their personalities. I knew what they liked. Their involvement in school-related activities strengthened their connection with their schools. They became closer to their teachers. They developed positive relationships with other students who were into positive things. Their behavior improved tremendously.

Building a meaningful relationship was different with the sister. When I first met the daughter, it was difficult to connect. A grown man does not have as much in common with a teenage girl as he does with young men. I had to really invest time in building a relationship before the sister started to open up. However, something that helped was, just like the younger brothers, as she saw the older brother's connection with me grow, she started to come around a little. It was a slow process, but it was a movement in the right direction. Something else I noticed was I didn't have to do as much to help her. I didn't enter her into programs or get her a job. Still, my presence in her life made a huge impact. Having a positive adult male figure in her life was transformative for her. What she really needed was to feel valued by a man she respected.

As a younger teenager, she had begun making the transition from a girl to a young lady. That can be a difficult time for any girl. She didn't see herself as beautiful. The reassurances a little girl gets from her father, she lacked because she didn't have a strong relationship with her father. My being around her, a positive male figure in her life, changed her opinion of herself. I also helped her brothers look at the words they used around her and be intentional about how they treated her. We all watched her transform right in front of us.

But right when it seemed like all the kids were in a much better place, I received a call from their mother. It was early that day, and she seemed extremely upset. Nothing could prepare me for what she was going to tell me. The stress of being a single mother was always overwhelming, but it had finally broken her. She called a government agency and told them she could no longer provide a safe home for her children. She was told they would be removed but kept together. She sincerely thought this was in their best interest, until the day came for her children to be removed.

I am not sure how the entire process went. What I do know is that the children were being removed separately. When the mother called me, all I heard was screams and crying in the background. The children were being ripped apart. The mother asked me to hurry over and try to stop what was happening. But there was nothing I could do. The papers had already been signed, and she admitted to not being able to care for them.

Building a Connection Can Be Scary— but Try Anyway

I told myself I would never let myself feel that again. I would never become connected to another child on that level. What made watching them go through so much pain so difficult was the connection we built with each other. They had become like family. I said I was done working with children all together—it just hurt too much.

But clearly, that is not how my story has played out. Watching their entire world be ripped apart hurt more than words can explain and they had an extremely sad outcome, but I had to ask myself a very difficult question: What would have happened if they were separated before I helped give them hope, helped them develop solid relationships with their teachers and school staff, introduced them to new circles of people, and helped them develop into better versions of themselves?

Building a connection can be scary. Connecting with people means change agents are opening themselves up. And change agents have to get close to build a connection. By getting close, change agents are allowing themselves to care. However, if something goes wrong, it can hurt.

A change agent could invest time and it could lead nowhere. Yes, a change agent can give their all—and get nothing in return. A change agent could become attached because they took the time to develop a deep connection, then watch the youth they're working with still fail. But what would happen if a change agent did nothing? The odds of failure, death, incarceration, a lifetime of trying to escape poverty, unemployment, and several other negative outcomes would be much greater if nothing at all is done.

Change agents face their fears. They have to invest the time. They have to let their guard down. They have to allow the youth they're working with to get close to them. Change agents have to get close to them as well. Change agents have to make the connection.

Developing a real connection is critical. If a change agent wants to truly change the way someone thinks and acts, they will need a relationship. Without a connection, they will not know them well enough to know how they think. A change agent has to be close enough to a person for them to let them inside.

The type of connection a change agent builds is important. It has to be built on the right foundation. It's not enough to simply be connected a change agent needs to be seen as trustworthy, authentic, genuine, relatable—and reliable. The relationship has to feel like a place where a youth can be themself without being negatively judged or pressured.

Lastly, change agents must open up first. They have to set the standard for the relationship. Change agents are the ones who will create the space they share with their youth. Regardless of what they get, change agents have to give the type of energy they want to receive. They have to break down the walls.

KEY FIRST STEP

Everything starts with having a genuine connection. People do not care how much you know until they know how much you care. Focus on letting the youth you are working with know you care and you are there for them. Look at the things the youth tells you from their perspective, not yours. Your goal is to understand why they think the way they do. Ask questions that give him or her the chance to explain why they feel, think, and act the way they do. If they told you they did something, ask why they did that. Follow up by asking how the experience made them feel, then ask if they would do the same thing the same way now—and allow them to fully explain.

The Importance of Consistency

Successful people do ordinary things
with extraordinary consistency,
commitment and focus.

—*Jon Gordon*

The presence of a change agent can be an extremely powerful force. A change agent can help a youth make critical transitions in their life and could be one of the most powerful tools a youth will ever have access to. A change agent's wisdom can be inspirational, create hope, give encouragement, help overcome fears, develop confidence, build new skills, and give exposure to a whole new world, among countless other things.

However, without consistency, a change agent is virtually ineffective. A lot of our highest-risk youth have experienced people going in and out of their lives all their lives. Many of them had parents who promised to make changes, like stopping committing crime or fighting substance addition, but they never delivered. Because they could not make the necessary changes, they were taken out of their child's life. Their parents may have broken their word to a point where it hurts less just to shut them out and not believe their promises than to keep hoping for a different outcome. Some youth may have grown up around adults, not just parents, who never honored their commitment to them.

Once a higher-risk youth opens up and lets a change agent in, that person matters to them. What the change agent does matters from that point on. If they say they're going to do something and do not follow up, all the trust they built could be lost. The bond they worked so hard to build could be broken just like that. Trust may never be regained. The willingness to trust, however, may not be lost just for that particular change agent.

Youth are stepping out on faith when they allow a change agent into their life. It takes bravery to believe a situation is going to turn out differently than it has in the past after being hurt. If their own family abused their trust, it is completely understandable for a youth to close themself off so they do not have to feel anything like that again.

What do you think happens when a change agent breaks down the walls a youth put up and then does the exact same thing other people did in the past? How would it make you feel if the person you thought saw something special in you and came into your life to be something you never had turned out to be just like everyone who ever disappointed you? You may feel like they didn't really care the way they claimed to. Remember, the youth was used to people letting them down or disappearing, but they thought someone was finally going to make them feel like they were a priority when a change agent came into their life. Instead, the change agent confirmed their belief about everyone and everything being the same.

According to the organization Youth Mentor, "there are 46 million young people, age 8 to 18, living in America. Sixteen million of them are growing up without a mentor. That's one out of every three young people who, outside of their family at home, don't have a trusted adult who they believe they can turn to for advice or guidance. Of these young people, 9 million face a variety of day-to-day challenges that put them at-risk for falling off track."

Not only do youth need mentors but they also need more than one mentor. In Rico Surridge's article "Why Having Multiple Mentors Can Provide a Valuable Breadth of Perspective," he states, "I tend to recommend people should have somewhere between three to five mentors." Having multiple mentors helps youth gain a wider perspective, learn a variety of tools, and see multiple ways to build their life. Each mentor has an opportunity to reinforce the positive messages a youth hears from their other mentors. The compound positivity begins to spread and becomes fact, instead of just a dream or message.

The danger of a change agent breaking the trust the youth had in them is that that youth may not trust anyone else. Now instead of one positive interaction opening doors for more mentors to come into their life, the youth could close that door altogether. This could easily leave a youth trapped in a space where all they have access to are the negative conditions that create the risks they face.

Most people think of consistency simply as showing up when you say you will (but much more is required than being present, even though that is a very big part of the process). Every successful program has to be clear about what it hopes to accomplish; it needs structure and set guidelines for how it will operate; determine how frequently it will make contact with that participant; set how long each session will last; clarify what will be done in each session; and be clear about what is expected from each session. Change agents have to be equally structured and intentional.

Change agents must also be consistent with the examples they set. The youth change agents work with are watching what change agents do at all times—how a change agent treats others, the way they carry themself, their personal beliefs, and the role they play in a change agent's daily life, down to the way they dress and present themself. All of this is being transferred and observed. Once a person becomes a change agent, it is critical they understand everything about them is a part of their experience with the youth they serve.

For example, over the years, I have watched young men and women I've mentored grow into adults, parents, husbands and wives, business owners, and so many other amazing roles. A lot of their behaviors model my own. They tell their children things I told them. I watch them build businesses using tools and practices I shared. Their personalities have so many traces of mine.

I influenced the way they think, do, and are. I learned to be very careful about what I allowed to influence me because I would pass that on to the youth I care about. If I watched TV shows that shifted my views, that would be picked up on later. If I did not check my own character, how could I possibly authentically talk to a youth about theirs?

I changed things about myself on every level that I could. I worked with a therapist to further my self-development. Once I truly understood how much of an impact I made on others, I knew I did not have a choice. My programs were only one level of impact I made. My lifestyle, personal habits, and behaviors were just as important.

Using Trust to Build Confidence

I worked with a group of young men who were all in the justice system years ago. We were preparing for them to speak at a huge event. This was the first time any of them had ever done anything like this, and at first, they were completely against it. The thought of standing in front of a large audience was horrifying.

They did not know me well. Before we could even start preparing for the program, I had to gain their trust. The first step was to simply be there and allow them to get to know me. When they saw that I was authentic and was not just there for one week, they started to let me in. The more we spent time together, the more they picked up on things I told them. Once they trusted me, I was able to bring in other people to speak with them. Since the young men trusted me, they trusted my circle.

On the day of the event, I saw everyone was nervous. I had a travel-size bottle of cologne on me and used it in front of them. I told them I was nervous as well, but I always used cologne before I spoke to a group for good luck. Since the cologne worked for me, they all used it right before we stepped out.

My consistency in their life allowed them to trust me. The way I treated them set an example not only for how they treated me but also for how they began to treat each other. Once they saw having a mentor added value to their life, they allowed me to bring more mentors into their lives. Finally, they watched what I told them I consistently did that helped me and they added that as a tool that could help them.

KEY FIRST STEP

Take a long look at your availability. What demands do you have on your life? How do you already spend your free time? Determine how much time you can dedicate to another person. What mental and emotional capacity do you have available to give? Once you've determined how you can show up in a youth's life, communicate that to them.

Gauging a Youth's Highest Risks

Find a great mentor who believes in
you, your life will change forever!

—*Bill Walsh*

I often work with very large groups of youth. It is common for a school to contract my agency to create programs for their entire student body. A superintendent may want us to develop programs for a cluster of schools. A commissioner may ask me to develop an initiative for youth throughout their entire county. However, my agency does not have the resources to get to know each youth personally. Sometimes, we may have an entire school year with youth, and other times, we only have that day.

I used to come into a city and hold speaking engagements then leave. I felt great after just about every program. Adults and youth seemed to be inspired by my story. They would use my life like a GPS: see where to go or what to avoid by listening to how my decisions impacted my life.

Regardless of what they learned, everyone typically got something, and it always seemed positive. The fact that I went from being a drug dealer who hurt people every single day, to giving people hope, I felt like I was walking in my full purpose.

A month or two after the speaking event, I'd check back on the youth I talked to. And to my dismay, I would get pretty much the same response each time: some youth were killed, arrested; others dropped out; gangs were still pulling students in; or something else horrible happened.

Why would the same thing keep happening? I had delivered a powerful message and shared what I believed to be life-changing tools and advice. For instance, we had talked about the power of decisions and how one wrong choice can change the course of your life. I had discussed how to set goals and create a realistic life plan. Conflict resolution, controlling your emotions, the dangers of drugs and gangs, the importance of education and training, and so much more. I couldn't understand. Was my message not powerful? Were the tools and advice less important than I thought?

People would consistently tell me, "That's just how it's going to be." I couldn't realistically expect to save every single person. Some youth were just going to fall short of what I wanted for them. But I didn't accept that! I didn't fly across the country more than a hundred times a year to watch the same outcome repeat itself. What was the point of any of this if youth still had the same negative outcomes everywhere I went? If my messages were so powerful and moving and the tools really equipped youth, what was the problem?

I thought back to my friends who were incarcerated with me. I reflected on the people who became addicted to the drugs we sold. The more I looked at what increased our risks, the more questions I had. I struggled to find out what caused us to make the mistakes we made.

Then it clicked: There would never be a single reason. Even though we all came from similar backgrounds and had somewhat similar situations, each of us was affected differently. Our circumstances and environment only played a part in why we did the things we did.

The Power of Identifying Risks

So, I completely changed the way I did my programs. I still couldn't work with every youth independently, but I could train each school or group I worked with a key strategy: how to identify and prioritize a youth's risks. I trained people on how to identify risks, and then rank them from most dangerous to least serious. I was able to gain a keen awareness of the highest risks and the most dangerous behaviors of each group. Now, I could develop a strong strategy. I knew exactly what we needed to discuss and why. When I check back in on groups now, the reports are completely different. Not only are more of the youth safe but they are also thriving. I started off inspiring people by sharing my story. Now I empower youth, so they can rewrite their own story!

As a youth change agent, similar to what I began teaching schools to do, you should create a strategy based on the risks the youth you're working with are facing and what is increasing their risks. Your strategy has to be based on each youth you work with. No two youths have the exact same risks. It may seem like youth are following the same path or have the same dangers. But, regardless of how much their actions and situations look alike, they are different people, so their risks are also different. Doing the following will help you assess the risks in a youth's life:

1. **Determine what someone's highest risks are by seeing into their life.** Learn how they live, what they do, and what life looks like for them. Identify their habits and most common behaviors. Once you understand what a person is actually doing, you can see what could be dangerous. You can also determine what is going to hold their life back. For example, the biggest risk could be environmental

because they live in a very dangerous community. It could be incarceration because they are in need of money and making really bad decisions or have a lack of respect for authority. They could have a lack of options in the future because they won't go to school and do not value education. It could be gang related because they are hanging out with people who are already affiliated with gangs.

2. **Understand what is causing them to do what they are doing and stopping them from doing the things they shouldn't do.** When you understand what is causing the person to be in danger, you can build a strategy on how to approach each risk. If they are unaware of their actions, you can explain the severity to them. If they have a situation that is placing them in danger, you can try to remove them from the situation or reach out to someone or an agency who can. For example, it could be as simple as asking a youth to stop going to a certain place you've both identified as unnecessarily dangerous. You may not be able to move them out of their home or community personally, but you may be able to talk their caregiver into allowing them to temporarily stay with a relative or while they go through a program. You may be able to help them change schools so they are in a better environment or have access to more resources.

If they are making extremely bad decisions or hanging with the wrong people, you know what to focus your conversation around. If they are in a bad place and forced to do things that will impact their survival, you can connect them with groups that provide the type of support they need.

3. **Gauge which of their actions places them at risk or puts them in the most danger.** You also have to know the probability of something bad happening due to each risk. Know the worst thing that could happen because of each risk. What could completely derail their future today or cause them to lose their life? Those are their highest risks—you have to address those immediately. If something is holding them back, but not increasing their likelihood of being here tomorrow, that is still important, but it's not the first priority. If they didn't live to graduate high school, a college scholarship isn't going to do them any good. Are they aware of their own risks? Do they understand how their actions place them in more danger? There is no way to know any of this until you really understand the youth's relationship with their risks.

Gauging the level of each risk is important because you cannot change their entire life or work on every risk factor at the same time. Prioritize what is most important. If the worst thing happens, could it change the course of a youth's entire life or does it only have the potential to cause a minor setback? Work on what could have the worst impact or cause the worst disruption. Determine whether a risk factor is something that is very likely due to their behavior and habits or current lifestyle.

Think of this assessment as your research. In the same way you would research a project, think of the youth you're investing your time and energy into as your passion project. You are passionate about their future. You're refusing to allow them to fail! You will take the time to build a genuine relationship and get to know them, so you get close enough to do the proper research and then build your strategy to help them.

How Understanding a Youth's Highest Risks Empowers Your Work in Their Life

Years ago, I was asked to host an event for some Georgia legislators. The event was centered around youth who battled with both substance abuse and self-harm challenges. This was a very important event because the commissioners, state representatives, city officials, and other politicians in attendance determined the budget that programs working in this space would receive. It was critical that everyone understood the impact programming made for these youth.

Having access to solid programs is life or death for many of the youth we were advocating for. I was tasked with not only explaining what thousands of children and young adults suffered from, but I also had to make sure that everyone understood their struggles and felt their souls.

But there are countless important areas of work and service. Political leaders serve everyone within their districts. In order to increase the budget in one area, money has to be taken from another area. If I did not articulate the pain high-risk youth felt, how overwhelming their struggles were, and why hope had been ripped away from many of them, someone could lose their life because the support they needed would not be accessible.

I had been working with a few dozen youth in a treatment facility for about a year prior to the event. I didn't work with them daily or even every week. Sometimes, I would see them once a week, and other times, it may have been once a season. The youth at the facility had all either attempted to hurt themselves or battled with serious substance addictions at some point.

I held programs at the facility, talked with the youth about my own struggles at different stages when life felt so dark that I thought about hurting myself, and I told them how I made it through that chapter. During our sessions, I let the group know there were times I felt like I was trapped. I was going back and forth to jail so much, it seemed like my life would never change. Once I lost hope,

I started questioning if not being here was the only way I could break the cycle.

Then I let them know I found a better way. I broke my cycle by believing in myself and forcing myself to dream. Once I could see my dream to the point where I believed in it, I did the work to make it my reality. The more work I did, the more things would change. I let them know the more I saw change, the more hope I was able to build. The more I felt hope, the more my life felt like it was not only worth living but also too valuable to harm.

The more I shared my own battles and struggles, the groups did as well. My honesty and transparency set the tone for our relationship. They were as real with me as I was with them. It got to a point where the group would talk about general things during sessions then people who didn't feel comfortable opening up with everyone would come back to speak one-on-one.

After a few months, our relationships were so solid, I could ask them anything. I let them explain why they needed drugs. I also asked things about the situations when they thought about hurting themselves. I asked how did they get to that point. Why did they believe hurting themselves was the solution to their problems? What triggered them? How did they actually try to hurt themselves? I even asked what they believed they needed that could help, but didn't have access to. I asked what they did throughout the day on a regular day, and then I asked what did they do if they were having a crisis or just weren't feeling it on a specific day.

I wanted to know and understand as much as possible about them. I needed to see into their life. I also wanted to understand how they thought and why. This was so important because the youth were going to be a part of the program I was holding. The plan was for us to speak to the crowd together. Their testimonies were the only thing that could touch the lawmakers' hearts and then move them to increase the amount of services and resources youth in this position had access to.

Speaking about the darkest moments in your life can be triggering. You are taking yourself back to that space when you open up. It can feel like you are reliving the worst moments of your life. The emotions can flood you all over again. The overwhelming pressure can cause the strongest person to relapse.

I was placing the youth at risk, but I was doing it for them. There was no way I could put a child in danger without understanding exactly what type of danger I was creating. It would be impossible for me to protect youth from something if I did not really understand the situation I was creating, and then see the way it impacted them from their perspective.

In order to prepare for the talk, we talked about everything personal in a one-on-one setting they were comfortable with. We did this until I could see exactly what could trigger each person. I also was able to determine what each youth could handle discussing and what they couldn't. I identified their triggers and what could possibly happen after they were triggered. Now I had to set limits on what each person could handle discussing. The last thing we had to do was come up with a safety plan, which allowed each youth to end a conversation if it pushed them into a place they didn't want to go to.

On the big day, we set up the event to feel like a television talk show. I was the host and two youths came out at a time, like they were my special guests for the night. Because we built such a good relationship and understanding, everyone felt good about talking with me about deep and personal things. The crowd was just there to listen in on our conversation and learn. I knew them, so I could visually see when they became uncomfortable or emotional. So, without them saying a word, I knew when to stop the entire conversation or switch the subject. I also knew when to put my hand on someone's back for comfort. I knew when to tell a joke instead of continuing with questions. I knew when to use myself as an example and then allow them to join in when or if they felt like they wanted to.

By the end of the event, there was not a dry eye in the entire facility. People learned more about our youth than they ever imagined. For the first time, the people who were tasked with making life-or-death decisions for our youth truly saw what it felt like to walk through life in their shoes. Instead of feeling vulnerable, every youth who participated was empowered. They saw how much power there was inside of them. I avoided all of their triggers and only touched on their areas of strength because I took the time to truly understand their risks beforehand. Not only did the youth secure the funding needed to change other people's lives but they also changed their own lives—they took back their power from things that once made them feel powerless.

KEY FIRST STEP

Your goal is to understand what the youth you're working with are doing that could hurt them. You want to know what their highest risks are. Listen with intention. Identify as many risks as possible then rank which are the most dangerous.

Helping Youth Understand Their Risks

A mentor is someone who sees more talent
and ability within you, than you see in
yourself, and helps bring it out of you.

—Bob Proctor

Do you recognize the name LaKeith Smith? Whether you
do or don't, I'm sharing his story because you should know
what happens when our youth do not have the type of positive support they need to truly understand the impact of the
decisions they make.

In 2015, a group of young Black men between the ages of fourteen and sixteen decided to go to a community close to theirs. They lived in Montgomery, Alabama, and they drove to a neighboring area in Elmore County. They went there to look at houses.

Why were the young men going so far from home, just to look at houses? They were not looking for just motivation. Some people find inspiration by admiring the neighborhoods and lifestyles of other people. Motivation was not enough for them. They wanted what the people there had. The boys went there to take what they saw.

Stealing is common on the long list of poor choices youth make far too often. At times, youth start to steal out of stores or they steal out of cars, and sometimes, they steal cars altogether. They may even steal out of people's homes. This is what LaKeith and his friends did. They wanted electronics they could sell easily, to make fast money.

When I was a little younger than them, I broke into my first home. I went into a house right up the street from my own with a group of friends, just like LaKeith. But I was extremely uncomfortable. I did not like the feeling. Looking through other people's belongings and trying to find anything of value, it was not for me. My friends, however, felt differently. For them, it was easy and quick money. In less than thirty minutes, they could be in and out with a few thousand dollars' worth of things to sell or more when they found the right house.

Things did not go as planned for LaKeith and his friends—not at all. One of the neighbors saw their car pull into a driveway and witnessed them go inside their White neighbors' home. A group of Black boys went into a White family's house alone. They also knew their neighbors were at work. So, they called the police.

When the police pulled up, the boys ran. They had guns on them when they broke into the house and probably did not plan to use them. But one of the boys turned around and fired a shot at a policeman while he tried to run away. The officers fired back. As a result, sixteen-year-old A'Donte Washington was shot. He would never see his seventeenth birthday. The officer's body camera footage showed that A'Donte was armed with a gun and that he was facing the officer when he shot at him. The shooting was found to be justified, and the officer was not charged for the killing.

LaKeith was not as fortunate. What started off as five young men breaking into two homes that afternoon would end very differently for him. LaKeith was found in the woods behind the house, hiding. He thought he was being arrested for breaking into the house, but he was wrong: he was arrested and charged with murder.

In the case of A'Donte, everyone knew who killed him. A police officer fired the bullets that killed A'Donte and the footage captured on the officer's body camera recorded it. How was LaKeith held responsible for a murder he never even saw take place? He was in the woods when the shots were fired. So, why would someone be arrested for a murder they did not commit?

Like almost all fifteen-year-old minority boys, living in a low-income community and growing up in single-family homes, LaKeith had a lower level of education. He had never heard of the felony murder law, a legal doctrine that holds someone liable for murder if they participate in a felony, such as a robbery, that results in someone's death. Currently, forty-eight states have felony murder laws. A'Donte was killed while committing a crime with four of his friends. As a result, all the other young men were held responsible for his death. In the eyes of the law, if they never committed the crime, no one would have lost their life.

LaKeith did not understand how he could be held accountable for an action he did not do. All the other young men took plea deals. They understood how their decisions led to the death of their friend, and for some of them, a cousin. LaKeith went to trial because he genuinely did not understand. He was found guilty and sentenced to sixty-five years. Now, almost ten years later, all the other young men have served their time and are back home.

In March 2023, a new sentencing hearing was held for LaKeith after a judge ruled that his original lawyer failed to present possible mitigating evidence about his home life and mental health. The judge sentenced the now twenty-four-year-old LaKeith to thirty years in prison—a reduction from the more than fifty years he originally received, but a blow to his family and advocates who argued he should not spend decades in prison for a killing he did not commit. Even A'Donte's father spoke up for LaKeith following the 2023 sentencing: "They were kids, just kids. I don't condone them going to somebody's house and whatever. Give them time for that. But the murder of my child? No," Andre Washington told reporters.

Over the years, I have watched countless youth make mistakes that completely changed the course of their life. For youth who already live with higher-than-normal risks, it is easier to derail their future. Think of it like a person who lives on a fixed budget. The tighter their budget, the less room they have for mistakes. If a person needs every single dollar to cover their bills and they misuse twenty dollars, they could struggle to have gas money to make it to work, or their lights could be turned off.

Youth who are closely connected to the dangers that change agents are working so hard to make sure they avoid do not have the luxury to make what could seem like simple mistakes. The wrong color shirt or hat. Walking down a dark street or even the same street they go down every single day, but at the wrong time. Going into a store with the wrong group of friends. Getting inside a car, but not checking to see exactly what is in the car first or if the car was stolen.

Any number of things could easily change a child's life. They could lose their life in seconds. They may experience something that traumatizes them, then be forced to live with that or through that. Even if they are not killed, they may never be the same again.

Because they live in a high-crime community, youth are expected to commit crimes. They did not pick the area they live in, but they are there, and so are police officers, looking for the next person to arrest. In low-income areas, unemployment is higher, as is poverty, which causes more people to commit crimes as a means of survival. Police are aware of this, so they patrol these areas more heavily.

Statistics show youth are watched more when they are minorities and when they live in poverty. According to a study by the ACLU of New York published in a report titled "A Closer Look at Stop-and-Frisk in NYC," "From 2003 to 2021 90 percent of people stopped by the NYPD were people of color." Black and Brown youth have a much higher risk of being accused of crimes, just because of the color of their skin. A report done by the Bureau of Justice Statistics titled *Lifetime Likelihood of Going to State or Federal Prison* stated, "Among men, more than 1 in 4 blacks and 1 in 6 Hispanics, compared to 1 in 23 whites, will enter prison at least once."

Just like many youths or adults do not know what felony murder is and how it can impact their lives, they also do not know their risks are so high, just because of the color of their skin and the community they were born in. They also do not know if they are in a car and a crime was committed, they can all be charged. One bag of a drug could be a felony for everyone. The same with a gun or anything illegal. One crime can easily be years of their life gone and a lifetime of being a convicted felon, even if they had no idea what was done before they got in the car or what was inside the car.

The risks do not begin or end here. What if a young man is walking through his neighborhood and stops to speak to a group of friends he went to school with? What if a young lady takes a few pictures with a group of friends she's known all of her life because they grew up together? This could easily turn into a gang charge. If one person out of the group is caught committing one crime, they could all be charged with a crime. That crime could be enhanced because it is connected to a gang. Wearing very similar clothes. Representing an area of a city they all grew up in. Doing the same dances or having a special handshake. All of these things could be very innocent youth behavior or it could be enough for a conviction.

When a youth has an attorney, many of the things I mentioned may not be that big of a deal. Even a decent attorney could get most of this dismissed. The problem is, even a decent attorney is unaffordable for many impoverished youth. How does a child who has struggled to eat and lives in poverty or close to it pay for any level of legal representation? Who do they have to turn to for help? Remember, their family struggled to provide the basics for them. Their community is struggling as well.

To the criminal justice system, minority youth can easily be seen as just another number. Even before they are found guilty or innocent, a person can sit in jail for years, just waiting to go to trial. The US Commission on Civil Rights stated within their report *The Civil Rights Implications of Cash Bail* that "more than 60% of defendants are detained pre-trial because they can't afford to post bail." This means all of these people are serving a sentence before being sentenced.

Most people also cannot afford to stay incarcerated or handle the conditions within correctional facilities. The Vera Institute of Justice stated, "97 percent in large urban state courts in 2009, and 90 percent in Federal Court in 2014 are adjudicated through guilty pleas" in their report, *In the Shadows: A Review of the Research on Plea Bargaining.*

This means people take guilty pleas just to get their freedom back. They may not be able to afford bond and a lawyer. People may have been overwhelmed by being removed from everything they knew and then thrown inside a cage, where they were forced to live twenty-four hours a day. Hours turn into days, then days turn into weeks, weeks to months, and months can turn into years. These people were never actually found guilty of anything. They could have just been the wrong color or gender, in the wrong area, born to the wrong family, with the wrong group of people, or in the wrong car at the wrong time. Regardless, they will have a conviction on their record for life. They may even lose years of their life or their entire life, depending on the charge. Remember, we are talking about youth and young adults. This can change their lives because all of this is happening during a critical time in their lives. This is the development stage for them.

It is a change agent's duty and responsibility to educate youth and young adults about the dangers they face. As a youth change agent, it is also your job to make sure the young person is aware of what can happen to them if they make one wrong decision. A person cannot avoid what they do not understand.

KEY FIRST STEP

It is not enough for you to understand a youth's risks. The youth you are working with needs to understand the most dangerous things in their life as well. Start openly discussing the various things they are around or doing that can negatively impact their life. Describe in detail what those various negative outcomes could look like.

The Importance of Self-Determination

We all have dreams. But in order to
make dreams come into reality, it
takes an awful lot of determination,
dedication, self-discipline, and effort.

—*Jesse Owens*

I am often asked, "How did you get the judge in your case to give you another chance?" What people don't realize is that before my judge or anyone could give me a chance, I had to give myself one. I had to give the judge over my case a reason to even consider giving me the opportunity to return back into society.

While I was out on bond from my last big drug charge, I went back to school. I began working also. I started a program right after I was released on bond at my local community college for marketing and accounting and completed it before I was sentenced. I also held down my job during the entirety of my case.

What is the point of being incarcerated? When you think about why people are given prison sentences after they commit a crime, what do you believe their punishment is intended to do? Incarceration has two main goals. The first is to separate dangerous people from innocent members of society. This is why violent crimes are given longer sentences. If a criminal uses violence in the commission of a crime or cannot control their actions, they have a higher likelihood of hurting someone. The second goal is for someone to learn from their actions and then change their behavior. This should happen after having enough time to truly reflect on their actions, be exposed to new things, and learn new tools or skills.

I rehabilitated myself. I did this while I was going through the trial process. I changed my environment by going to college. I also moved away from my old neighborhood so I could get time alone to really reflect on my life. Instead of selling drugs, like I did for the last fifteen years, I started working and earned a living legally. I did not just get a job—I started building a career.

I took the initiative to invest in myself even though the possibility of a lengthy prison sentence was hanging over my head. I did all of this on my own and without support. I invested in myself and learned a trade so I could build workable skills. I also changed my mindset by educating myself.

The same judge who gave me a chance sentenced hundreds of men who looked like me, came from similar backgrounds, and committed the same crimes. He sent them to prison. Actually, we all sent ourselves to prison; we were the ones who broke the law. The judge did his job, but our actions placed us in the courtroom and in the position to be sentenced. The judge did his job countless times before my case was in front of him, and he continued to do his job after me.

What was different in my case was that I allowed the judge to see the person I had the potential to be. More importantly, it was clear to him that I saw the person I could be. I proved that I wanted to be more and better. My actions showed that I was ready for a change, and I would do the work to become a better man.

Why is this so important? The only way the youth a change agent is working with will successfully change their life is if they believe in the potential within themself. No matter how much the change agent believes in them, they have to believe in themself. They have to want it. If they don't want to grow or change, it will be very difficult to help them change. Growth takes work, and a change agent cannot do the work for them.

Investing in someone is simply multiplying their effort. If they have zero effort, it's no different than multiplying anything by zero. Ten times zero is zero. One million times zero is still the same, zero. The determining factor for the equation is the same—zero effort will always produce zero outcome.

This is another reason why hope is so critical. A person with no hope is going to have zero to give toward their future. How can you invest in a future you don't believe in? If a person does not believe things can change or be better, why would they try? No matter how much a change agent attempts to help them make changes, they won't accept the change agent's help. If they do, they won't do their part to actually make the transformation.

I sold drugs for fifteen years. I did not believe I could make it without selling drugs. I thought the only way I could survive was by hustling. Since I wholeheartedly believed this, it became my reality. No matter what someone did for me or how much they wanted to help me, I would always go back to what I believed in. No one could be successful at reaching me, no matter how much they tried, because I completely bought into the fact that I had to be a drug dealer.

A change agent cannot free someone from something they won't release. Before a change agent can work on changing behaviors, they have to change the youth's beliefs. A person's beliefs are much more deeply rooted than most of us realize. Our beliefs guide our actions, morals, ethics, and norms. Everything we do is motivated by something we believe.

Growing up, we had very few food choices in our community. We had a fast-food burger place at one point, but it closed after multiple people were killed in the parking lot in a short period of time. We also had a pizza chain restaurant, but it also closed after it was robbed over and over. We had a restaurant that sold fried chicken, which we all ate pretty much daily. When I was almost thirteen years old, a hot-wing restaurant opened. I was the first customer. Chicken was my favorite food because I ate mostly chicken. The thought of chicken served in more than a dozen flavors was like heaven to me. Now, after I've experienced food from around the world, I've come to realize I do not like hot wings or fried chicken nearly as much as I thought I did. In the hood, we are forced to eat certain foods because it's all we have, but you never really know what you do or don't like if you've only had limited exposure.

A few years later, I opened a barbershop in our neighborhood and a car detailing shop. A fish restaurant right up the street from both of my businesses decided to support me. The restaurant was a chain and very popular. I had flyers printed for my companies, one on each side. They put my flyer in every bag when someone ordered food. Because they supported me so heavily, I ate there at least three times a week. One day, I was in an upscale neighborhood out of town. I was slightly uncomfortable because I felt out of place. I saw the same restaurant as the one in my neighborhood, so I went there since it reminded me of home. I ordered the same exact side dish (broccoli) with my meal. However, I took it back twice because something was wrong. The second time, I had a slight attitude. I told them that the broccoli was hot, and everyone gave me a strange look. But actually, it was meant to be served hot. For years, I only had it from the restaurant in my neighborhood—it was never hot. I had grown so used to that I had no idea it could be served differently or was being served incorrectly based on the restaurant's own standards.

Most of our beliefs were given to us; we didn't create them for ourselves. What we hear other people say influences our beliefs. If our parents say it, if our peers believe it, if our culture embraces it, we most likely will believe it as well. As a result, we have countless beliefs that we are not aware of, and many of these beliefs don't serve us well. We do not see the damage our beliefs may be causing us because we aren't even aware of them. Even if we are, we may not know anything else, so we think what we believe is the only way to think.

I thought the only way I could make it out of poverty was by being a criminal. I saw people go to work every day. Many of those people worked extremely hard. But no matter how hard they worked, nothing in their life changed. They could work until they were near collapse from being tired, and their lights would still get cut off and their children would be hungry. At the same time, I saw young dudes who sold drugs with their friends, and they all ate whatever they wanted whenever they wanted to. Even if someone in the neighborhood had a good life and worked legally to build it, I didn't see them because they were at work or in their house.

My father worked, and he made good money. But I wasn't close to him. At a young age, I didn't understand what my father did. We lived in the house together, but he was extremely violent. I avoided him. It's hard to look up to the man who abuses your mother, even if that man is your father. So, many of the lessons I should have gotten from him, I couldn't receive them. I knew I didn't want to be like him, so I took away very little from him.

The streets, on the other hand, embraced me differently than anything or anyone in my life did. The streets had room for me. I didn't have to force the streets to notice me. The streets gave me a family, a home; no other association did that. The people in the streets treated me with respect, and I watched them be respected by everyone, so having their respect meant a lot.

The guys in the streets were rough, but happy. My father was violent and angry. Everyone else was struggling and stressed. It seemed like the only way to not be stressed was to have money. The only thing left in my mind was to be a drug dealer. I made this decision before I finished elementary school.

The first step is to find out why the person a change agent is working with won't release what is harming them or placing them in danger. Once they understand that, then the change agent can start the process of being transformative in a child's life. The reason a judge chose to let me walk freely back into society, without being overseen by a probation or parole officer, is because he saw that I had already made the decision to let go of the beliefs that kept me chained to being a criminal from the age of twelve years old to almost thirty.

KEY FIRST STEP

No matter how much someone believes in a youth, if the youth does not believe in themself, it won't matter. The youth you are working with has to be totally invested in their dreams and goals. You need to explain how important it will be to do the work and stay committed until they see the changes they want in their life, and the work has to start with them. Doing the right things, working hard, and being passionate about their future have to become a part of who they are.

Gaining Skills to Decrease Risks

Even the simplest tools can empower
people to do great things.

—*Christopher Isaac "Biz" Stone*

Whether I'm speaking to a group or the media, I seem to get asked the same questions: What happened in my life to cause me to stop selling drugs after so many years? Why did I finally change?

Everyone seems to want a short and to-the-point answer. If there is a cheat code, I do not know it. My response is usually a lot different than what people expect. There was not one single thing that caused me to change my life, though, or that made changing my life possible—there were several things that happened that made me see the way I was living was not right. I wanted something different for years, but I was unaware of what *different* actually meant, and no one was there to show me, plus I had no idea how to find out what I needed to change and then actually start the process.

Change is complex. Usually, change happens in stages. We have discussed why change is important, how to motivate change, and how to create an environment that makes change possible. I had the desire to change long before I had the capability to actually make it happen. For years, I wanted something different and to be different. I didn't know exactly what the change I needed to make looked like. Looking back, I now know I lacked the tools, exposure, support systems, and even the motivation to actually successfully make a change.

I did not complete high school, so I did not have a solid educational foundation. I did not have enough positive exposure, so I didn't know what a positive lifestyle or behavior really looked like outside of low-income inner-city communities. I normalized a lot of things that were extremely toxic because I was so accustomed to them. For example, I had no clue how to build a career or earn a living legally. I was around crime and violence as far back as I can remember, so all of the negative lessons I learned were engraved into my mind so deeply it was subconscious.

Before our youth are old enough to gain access to the world and challenge these beliefs by seeing how other people live, the problems have already started. According to the National Institute of Justice, in their report *The Age-Crime Curve*, the prevalence of offending tends to increase from late childhood, peak in teenage years (from fifteen to nineteen), and then decline in the early twenties. The average age of onset is earliest for gang membership (average age of 15.9), followed by marijuana use (16.5), drug dealing (17.0), gun carrying (17.3), and hard drug use (17.5).

In short, the average person begins their pattern of bad decisions while they are just children. By the time they become adults, the damage is done. Our highest-risk youth may not make it to adulthood. If they do, they may already be in prison or gang-involved. They may already be addicted to drugs or have started making a living by selling them. However, the studies show that if a person remains out of trouble by their early twenties, their risks are tremendously reduced. Intervention is very powerful and important because change agents can help youth regain control over their life, but prevention stops the negative actions before they start.

The Impact of Influences on a Youth's Life

Our youth are slowly conditioned from the day they are born. During the developmental stages, the environment a child grows up in and the behavior that is modeled has a huge impact on them. They learn countless ways to process, address, approach, and respond to different situations.

Similarly, youth who have problematic behavior were exposed to conditions that taught them to act that way. They could have picked up these things from the music they listen to, TV shows they watch, or social media influences. They hear and see this repeatedly on a daily basis, and they hear it for years. Their friends are being molded the same way or by very similar messages. This creates credibility, and they buy into the messages more and more as they see it reinforced. Their peers accept it as well.

For example, let's spend some time talking about the influence of music and social media. Remember, these are children who have not seen the world or had their own life experiences. They hear music created by people who look like them and come from similar backgrounds. They even share many of the same struggles. Now, those people are rich and famous, so they must be doing something right. People on social media have everything everyone else wants and are living the life other people dream about. They are popular and always seem happy. Not only have these people achieved the type of success our youth want, but they also usually did so while still young and made it all look so realistic, easy, and believable.

The influence shifts from being something they just hear and see via media and music to what they witness in real life. As they grow, their entire social circle picks up these influences. Now, the people around them start walking and living what they have studied. The way they dress, the words they use, what they see as success, their goals—every part of their culture is a product of what they have absorbed.

The child is now completely living what they were once only listening to and watching. But not only them—their entire peer group is doing the same things. This has become their culture. The more they accept and exhibit what is popular within their culture, the more they are rewarded. They become seemingly more popular themself, and the praise serves as positive reinforcement. The more they receive this praise, the more they dive into their pattern of behavior until all of this becomes a fixed belief system, which will become more and more difficult to break.

Creating a New Vision and Exposure Opportunities

Youth need exposure and visibility to a world outside of their own to be successful. Why did I keep doing the same things I saw that caused each of my friends to lose their life? Watching people just like me being murdered for doing the same exact things as me—it is the most hurtful and horrifying thing I have ever lived through. I felt hopeless and wanted a better life. I decided it would be better to be dead than to live trapped in poverty for the rest of my life. What was the point of being alive if I was forced to live a life where I was poor, hungry, and never had access to any of the things I wanted?

So, why wasn't losing my freedom enough motivation to change? Prison is only a threat when you feel like you are not already in one. When you are born into a toxic home, in a dangerous community, then forced to live around violence and crime, you are already in a prison. The only difference between hopelessness and a jail cell is that one has bars and walls.

If someone only knows one way to do something, that is what they are going to do. The odds of someone accomplishing a goal are very low if they cannot clearly see their goal or the route to success, which is why creating a clear vision and a thorough plan is critical.

So, what did I need but didn't have access to that kept me from being able to change my life? My vision was the beginning of my problems. I saw the world as a negative place, where you have to do whatever it takes to survive and make your way in. What I needed more than anything was a positive vision I could believe in and buy into. A positive vision would have stopped the entire process before it started because all of the negative actions would not have aligned with the positive mindset built around my vision.

The next thing I needed was exposure. Exposure reinforces what is possible. Without exposure, youth will believe the only thing that is possible is what they have seen. If they have only seen the world as hard and a place where you have to do anything to survive, that is exactly what our youth will do. If our youth are able to see a world outside of theirs, a place where people survive without having to commit a crime and are relatively happy, our youth will know they can live that way too. I also needed genuine connections with positive people so there would have been enough constructive things spoken into my ear to offset the influence of the music, media, and all the other toxic influences.

The Impact of Incarceration

One of the most important things I needed was the tools to survive in society without being a criminal. The tools to earn a living legally. No matter how much a person wants to stop doing illegal things, if that is all they know, what are they going to change to? We can only do what we know. Until we are taught something different, the odds of doing positive things are low to impossible.

A few years ago, I was teaching a program for a court. I served time in the same county the court was located in. I was convicted by the same court, in that exact courtroom. The same judge and district attorney who asked me to speak to young adults on their behalf were the same people who found me guilty and then sentenced me.

The program we were operating is called an alternative sentencing program. The goal of these types of programs is to reduce the likelihood of someone committing another crime by explaining the full consequence of their actions and then providing the needed support to make better decisions. Judges and prosecutors use these programs when they do not want to completely disrupt someone's life.

A conviction and incarceration can both have the opposite effect of what the justice system wants. The criminal justice system is designed to identify people who are threats to society and remove them to keep the rest of society safe. A felony conviction or being incarcerated can actually place society at greater risk by causing even more barriers for the person than they faced before.

The average person who is sent to prison is going to be released and return to society at some point. Only about 5 percent of the incarcerated population will remain in prison for the remainder of their life. This means almost every single person we send off to prison will return back to the communities, cities, and homes they were removed from. If these people do not learn new tools, they will return the same way they left and then possibly do the same things they did before.

When people are removed from their lives, it can be extremely challenging for them to get their life back on track. Sending someone to prison, taking years of their life away, and separating a person from everything they have is not a decision to be made lightly. That one action can completely change the rest of a person's life, plus the lives of everyone connected to them.

When you are sent to prison, you typically lose everything you have. Your job. Your house. Your car. Your savings. Any goals you had. Even hope and motivation. All of that could be snatched away with one conviction, even from a short prison sentence.

Not everyone who commits a crime is a hardened criminal. Some people are dangerous, and other people may be in a dangerous position. The professionals in the criminal justice system have to work hard, or at least they should, to determine who is who. A wrong decision can put an extremely dangerous person back into a community, placing community members in danger. For someone else, a bad situation or just life's pressure could have pushed an already desperate person to do something extremely bad. A person already fighting to survive through a hard situation could decide to commit a crime, thinking it could help them. What do you think that person may do after they lose their job after being incarcerated and then they cannot find another job as a result of having a felony conviction placed on their criminal record?

An alternative sentencing program is a very powerful tool. When operated correctly, it can give a person access to the resources they need to build an entirely new set of tools and allow them to grow, instead of placing them inside of a prison. For my last and largest drug conviction, I went before a judge who believed in rehabilitation over incarceration, when possible. During my trial, my judge was made aware that I attended a community college, plus I learned a trade that allowed me to secure the first well-paying career-level job I ever had. I did all of this while I was out on bond.

The judge saw that I already had the tools I needed to survive in society without being a threat to anyone.

Guilty or innocent, that was not what the judge over my case had to determine—I was guilty of every single crime. The judge's job was figuring out what to do with me. I could have been forced to serve twenty years, easily. At the time, I was about twenty-five years old. I would come home at around forty-five. So, I would be coming back older and with less opportunity.

If I was willing to sell drugs at the age of twenty-five, what would I be willing to do at the age of forty-five? If I kept guns on me to protect my drugs even while I had money, what would I do with a gun as a forty-five-year-old man who had nothing and was struggling to get my life back together after being gone away for twenty years, especially when I was coming back with nothing but resentment?

Was it the best idea to stop all the momentum I made? Did it benefit society to sit me in a cage for twenty years? Would it be best to invest in the person I could possibly be? With the right support and access to new tools, who could I become?

As a result of the judge making what I believe was the right decision, you are reading a book I was able to write about reaching and helping youth change their life because I have spent the last fifteen years working with the highest-risk youth and young adults around the nation, instead of spending that same time sitting inside of a prison.

I do not think it is just important for youth to learn new skills—it is essential if they truly want to change their life. I have no doubt that investing the time and resources needed can enhance someone's likelihood of becoming a better person. I am a living proof of what can happen after a person learns, grows, and is given a chance—a chance to change. And change agents can help make that happen.

New Skills for a New Chance

A child who grew up in a dangerous environment or with a lack of resources developed skills that helped them to survive and thrive within that system. Those skills can limit their ability to thrive outside of that space. They could have been forced to do certain things so they were not the next person shot, beaten, or robbed just walking down the street or trying to make enough money to eat. For them to modify their behavior, they have to unlearn those mechanisms and learn new things to replace them with.

For example, it took me several years to find alternative ways to deal with threats or danger. As a younger child, if you did not fight when threatened, the rest of the neighborhood saw that you would not defend yourself, so then people would take advantage of you. When older, those same people would rob you and many robberies would end with someone being shot and killed. I removed myself from that environment by first changing who and what I allowed around me, then later by moving outside my community while I was out on bond and fighting for my freedom. I had to learn that the same thing that protected me before now placed me in danger because the same rules did not exist in my new environment. I could not simply stop because I saw this was wrong; the tools I used kept me alive for years. I had to learn a new way to address conflict and threats.

Indeed, many of the tools they have developed are toxic and can get them in trouble. If a person is going to successfully change their life, they have to gain access to new tools. Tools that reduce risks instead of increasing them. Tools that lighten their burdens instead of adding to them. Tools that open doors in their life instead of closing them. And change agents have to help develop these tools in an array of areas.

Change agents and youth have to understand the importance of job training and earning an education for the youth they work with. These skills reduce the dependency on dangerous illegal activities for basic survival. If youth cannot work, they will be forced to do something when they are in need. Youth also must have healthy communication and conflict resolution skills. If youth do not know how to communicate or resolve conflict in a healthy way, they will constantly have issues with others. To successfully accomplish this, they have to learn ways to address conflict without violence. As long as they only know one way to address a threat and eliminate it to keep themselves safe, they are going to continue to fight.

Many of the young people change agents work with have been taught to yell to be heard, to act up to be seen, to intimidate others to avoid being bullied, and to lie so they aren't unfairly punished, among other things. Each one of these is a tool they have developed to survive within their ecosystem. Change agents must be intentional about identifying each negative tool, explain why this method is problematic, and then replace the negative tool with a positive one.

Soft skills and life skills are equally important; these are essential tools everyone must gain as we grow into adulthood. For example, critical thinking tools and the ability to process and then find solutions for complex problems will change a youth's life by allowing them to resolve problems before they get out of hand.

What kept me from changing my life? Why was I trapped in the streets for fifteen years? I never developed the tools needed to be anything other than a drug dealer. I started selling drugs at the age of twelve and I continued until the age of twenty-seven. All I knew how to do was sell drugs. I could not read and barely learned anything because I never attended school. While my classmates were excited about going to high school, I was excited about buying my first eight ounces of weed. While they planned their college tour, I was serving a sentence for drug possession with the intent to distribute. Everything I was told over and over as a child was that the only way to become successful was by making it in the streets. I started paying a mortgage plus utilities in the ninth grade. My beliefs were drilled into my head. All the tools I developed were centered around the life I lived at the time and what I believed I had to do to survive.

KEY FIRST STEP

Without the necessary tools, change is not going to happen. But with the right tools, anything is possible. Start identifying the negative tools a youth needs to release and what positive tools they will need to gain.

Why YOU and the Hope You Bring Matter

> The nice thing about hope is that you can
> give it to someone else, someone who needs
> it even more than you do, and you will find
> you have not given yours away at all.
>
> —*Maya Angelou*

In a documentary news special I was asked to be part of, I made a statement that I hope resonated:

> *Our kids are not terrorists. They're not horrible people. They're misguided. They're lost. They're abandoned. They're alone. All I'm asking is for us to just commit to*

loving people. You know why? That youth who you don't reach might be the youth who ends up dead tomorrow.

I worked with a high school in an area close to where I grew up. Our relationship started years before there was a Making the Transition, Inc. Someone I knew was a teacher at the school. One day, I asked, "How can I help?" I did not have any plans or intentions. I simply wanted to assist in some kind of way. If she told me the school needed people to pick up trash around the property or to paint, I would have been walking around with a trash bag in my hand and a paintbrush in my pocket.

She knew my background. She also watched me speak with youth a few times and witnessed how the things I said were received. The young people seemed to respect the way I talked with them and valued the knowledge I shared. I would randomly stop and talk to young people all around my neighborhood. If I saw guys hustling in front of a store, I would pull in and casually start a conversation. If I saw young ladies doing something I knew would cause a problem for them later, I would ask if they minded me speaking with them. When circles of youth would be walking down the street, it was normal for me to get out of my car and walk with them, just to talk. The more I did this, the better our relationships would become and the easier it was to figure out how to talk with each group.

The results of my actions were pretty consistent. There would be smiling and laughing, which is always a good sign. But more than anything, the youth listened. At some point, there would be this moment that was like a light bulb turning on. I would share something and it would change the group's perspective.

My friend told me I could help and add value to the students at her school. She did not want me to bring a trash bag even though there was trash that needed to be cleaned up. She felt like any volunteer could help give the students a much more beautiful environment, which was important, but she wanted me to do something only a few people could do.

Instead, I was tasked with helping the students who thought they wanted to try out illegal activities think more deeply about their decisions. I could speak from a unique position. Since I started my journey into criminal activity at such a young age, I could speak from the ignorance of a youth's perspective and then with the wisdom of an adult who experienced everything they didn't know about. This was something her school did not have access to but needed. A high percentage of their students were becoming increasingly interested in the fast money they could be making by doing what seemed like simple crimes. The more I came to the school, the more teachers and other staff members would connect with me, and we built relationships. Other teachers began reaching out for me to speak with their classes.

One day, I received a call. This request was different than what I became used to. I was not being asked to speak to a class or at the school. The teacher wanted me to do an intervention with a young man they were afraid they lost.

The student had transferred to the school after his older brother was killed. Their family had moved to Atlanta from out of state. His older brother provided for their entire family: four siblings, including their brother, plus his two children; two more children by his younger sister; and their grandmother. She was older and had health challenges, so she was able to put their home and utilities in her name, but she was not able to work.

Now that the older brother was dead, someone had to provide. The student they wanted me to talk to was the person who stepped up. He was the oldest male now. He started walking in his brother's shoes. His brother sold hard drugs before his murder. Now the student decided to do the same. He could not find another way to make enough money to provide for that many people at such a young age.

The entire staff at the school was worried about him. Before he stopped coming to school, he played sports and had pretty good grades. He was a good student. Everyone knew his situation, but they did not know what to do. It was like the entire school was stuck watching a bad story being written, but they could not change it. The teachers believed I was their best hope for him.

I called and asked if I could take him to dinner. We had never met before this. I picked him up from his home and took him to a nice restaurant near his neighborhood. I did not want to take him too far because, like I said, he did not know me. We did not have a bond or any trust yet. We ordered, but neither one of us really ate. We talked instead. I shared my story with him, to let him know I understood the pressure of paying a mortgage and bills as a child.

He opened up to me after he saw our similarities. For hours, he told me everything he held in because there was never anyone else to talk to. He was just as afraid of his future as everyone else. He saw what happened to his brother, and he clearly saw how easily that could be him. What choice did he really have though? There were children in their house and someone had to make sure they ate.

After a few hours, I noticed he had tears in his eyes. I asked what the problem was. He was not emotional because of what we had talked about. Their family came from a very rough background, so it took more than his current situation to bring those types of emotions out of him. He was crying because he was touched by the fact that I listened to him. Never in his life had another man showed concern for what he felt.

Our bond was built. I asked if he would do me a favor like I did for him. The favor was for him to spend one week living like the other students in his family. It was prom season. I asked if I could pay his bills and send him to the prom. Everything he needed, I would cover. All I wanted him to focus on was being a high school student. He agreed.

As a result, he started going back to school. That summer, he graduated. We decided that he should join the military. This way, he could still provide for his family and continue earning an education. The plan worked. He felt like his future was bright and promising. So did I. Then a problem arose. He was released from the army because of a medical issue none of us knew he had. Once he was released, I helped him get into a small college. However, the problem with this was he was not being paid for going to school. He could not help his family while he was in school.

He started back hustling. I tried everything to find another solution. No one would give him a job. No non-profit organization would help his family. No matter how many calls I made or organizations I went to, I couldn't get assistance for him.

He was hustling, but he never stopped going to college; he did not miss one single class. My belief in him gave him hope. He matched my energy. I worked extremely hard to find a solution that would get him off the streets, and he stayed prepared. Because his siblings and all the children in their family were watching, it was life or death to break the cycle that took his brother away. He went to school about an hour away, but he would come back to the city to make money and then would go back to school. This was his routine.

However, everything was about to change. One day, he was meeting a group of young men back in the city to sell them drugs. The young men paid for the drugs, but they did not plan on letting him keep the money. When he walked away, they pulled out guns. One of them rushed him to take their money back. They started fighting, and the gunman dropped his weapon. The other gunman started shooting, and the young man I was working with shot back, killing both of the robbers.

This ended all the work we were doing. Because drugs were involved, this was a crime. There is no self-defense when committing a crime in our state. He was charged with murder. Now he is serving twenty-five years. His younger brother attempted to step up, just like he did when their older brother died. The younger brother was killed in another drug deal before my mentee was even sentenced. Now, the only living, unimprisoned male in their family is his child, who is under five years old. All of the other males have either been killed or are in prison.

If I had access to other youth change agents and a network, we would have found a job for him. If he had just one opportunity, everything may have been different. Three young Black men may still be alive now. Another young man would be in college instead of a prison. A family would not have been destroyed.

A network of youth change agents can save and change lives, redirect a youth's future, and create opportunity where there is none. Even though he is incarcerated, my mentee has earned multiple certificates and is working on a degree so he can legally provide for his family once he has the chance to. His life went in a completely different direction than expected, but he never gave up hope. We must never give up hope for any of the youth we work with either.

KEY FIRST STEP

The work you are doing is critical. You may be the first and only person to invest in a youth's life at this level. It is also important for you to work with a team. We can do more working together. Find other people who care about youth and are doing work to help them. Connect with people who can help youth in areas you cannot and offer to help where you can for others.

Development Exercise

This is an exercise I challenge every youth change agent to do prior to entering into a new relationship with any youth.

Every youth needs to be thoroughly educated, well-trained, and fully developed. The school system is designed to focus on both education and training. As change agents, we can assist a youth in both areas, but we are not entering their life to be tutors or to provide specific training to help youth enter the workforce. We can be partners with a youth's school. We can also connect with service providers who offer specific training opportunities. Change agents are not educators though.

When it comes to development, that is a different story. A change agent may be the only person in a youth's life who is fully committed to their development. It is our job to make sure every youth has the proper support needed to grow into a mentally and emotionally healthy, functional, well-prepared, hopeful, and happy young adult. A change agent may be the only person a youth has access to who is totally focused and committed to their development in this way.

Change agents have a unique opportunity. We are positioned perfectly to change the direction of a young person's life by helping them transition at a critical time in their life. Change agents have the ability to pave a road that leads a youth to greatness!

The school will have its goals for the youth you work with. The court system will have goals. The community has goals. Their parents and family will have goals. The youth will have their own goals. Change agents also need to have goals as well.

What does a fully developed youth look like? What should a youth possess once they are mature and ready to face the world alone? What should be different when a youth is released compared to when their change agent came into their life?

These are additional exercises; I want you to write out the following:

1. Write twenty-five experiences you had a child, then explain how each experience helped you grow and what you learned. This will help you remember what helped you develop as a youth.
2. If you defined development in your own words, how would you define it?

3. What does it mean to help a youth develop to you?
4. How would you list the characteristics of a fully developed youth?
5. What are five things a fully developed young adult should possess?
6. What separates a well-developed young adult from their peers?
7. What are three things you can do as a change agent to help a young person develop?
8. What are three things you need assistance with from other change agents to help a youth fully develop?
9. Give three examples of areas of development you struggled with as a youth.
10. What are three ways you wish someone helped you develop when you were the same age as the youth you are working with?
11. How do you believe your life would be different now if you were fully developed as a youth?

Now look at your network and think about who can help you accomplish the development goals you set for the youth you are working with. It truly takes a village to properly help a youth grow into a successful and productive member of society.

Resources and Tools

MTT.university
Our online university offers digital workshops, courses, and programs focused on risk reduction, behavior modification, life enrichment, character development, brain mapping, vision building, conflict resolution, and other critical areas of development.

YouthChangeAgent.com
Connect directly to the Youth Change Agent Network. You will find resources here to help you grow as a youth change agent. Connect with other youth change agents across the nation and globe. Build your tribe of youth change agents and impact change in your community. Become the best youth change agent possible.

MakingTheTransition.org
Here you will find powerful tools like our youth assessments, designed to help you connect with youth and identify their risks as thoroughly and quickly as possible; our private youth social connection platform; as well as our podcast, where we discuss all the topics related to helping our youth Make the Transition.

About the Authors

Keith Strickland is the founder and CEO of Making the Transition, Inc. (https://makingthetransition.org/), a behavioral modification and life enrichment agency working with inner-city youth and young adults.

Keith almost ruined his entire life before he had a clue what life was about or what he had the potential to be. He grew up in a community where he saw more homeless people and hustlers than dual-parent households and professional adults. After years of overwhelming influence, he started to think the illegal activity he saw daily was normal.

His first arrest was for shoplifting from a local store when he was still in middle school. Directly after that, he started selling drugs—he was about thirteen years old. When he first started high school, he could tell that his life was out of control and leading him in a direction he did not want to go in. He did not know what to do or how to change though. He looked for a mentor, but there were no organizations or people who offered the type of assistance he needed.

He was arrested at his high school after being caught with a large amount of money and drugs. He would never attend high school again. He was now an independent adult who could barely read but knew how to sell drugs and survive as a criminal. Every influence he had pulled him deeper in the direction he once tried to run away from. By the time he turned twenty-five, he had been arrested over fifty times, watched hundreds of people be murdered, was kidnapped and then left for dead in a robbery, and served almost five years of his life behind bars.

He was given an opportunity most people in his position never receive: a second chance. After facing thirty-five years in prison for another drug conviction, he was released early because the judge over his case saw something in him. He started a business, went to college, earned his degree, and was able to finally get his life on track. Saving his own life was not enough for him. Every single day, he watched millions of youth and young adults on the exact same path he escaped from. He founded Making the Transition, Inc. because he never wanted another child who tried to change their life to fail because they lacked resources, guidance, and support.

He is dedicated to preventing them from taking the wrong paths he took. And for those who may have, give them a chance to get it right, a chance he was given. Through

Making the Transition, Keith has developed courses, workshops, and programs that are taught in schools across the nation, impacting the lives of more than a hundred thousand youth and young adults. He was a consultant to the Obama administration and has been asked to do the same by the Biden administration.

In May 2022, Keith received an honorary doctorate from Carver University, an HBCU in Atlanta, for his work in the community and dedication to the advancement of youth. Says Keith of that achievement: "I went from a high school dropout to having a doctorate. Tell me God isn't real!"

Keith has purchased all the properties on a now abandoned street where he once sold drugs to build a community school, a research center, and a training facility focused on inner-city youth development, as well as a community park.

Lucas L. Johnson II is a former reporter for The Associated Press, where he worked for more than twenty years mainly covering politics, education, and prison reform. He also authored the book *Finding the Good*. First published in 2003, it was rereleased by HarperCollins in 2021. Lucas works in higher education and has taught high school and college students. He lives in Nashville, Tennessee.

Acknowledgments

I would like to express my gratitude to God for believing in me long before I ever believed in you. All the mistakes I've made. The years I sold to people you loved the drugs that kept them trapped in a vicious cycle. The youth I gave the wrong examples to. The shootings that caused innocent people to live in fear. All of my closest friends who died along the way. The prison sentences you released me from. The multiple times I should have been killed. The motorcycle and car wrecks that could have completely changed the way I live today. All the years I hurt so many people. You still saw something in me that was worthy of not only saving but also lifting to heights I never imagined. When I could not find a job, you gave me a company. When I could not secure funding, you gave me contracts so I could build something big enough to provide for thousands of youth. At times, it's hard to remember that I learned to read by trading my food to another inmate for weeks, and now, I'm a published author who uses the gift you blessed me with to reach youth who are in the exact same positions I was once in—before the world gets a hold of them and they make the same mistakes I made. You took me from being homeless and sleeping on people's floors and sofas and then renting rooms that I paid for with drugs. When I refused to sell another drug or do anything that would hurt another person, I had no idea how I would provide for myself. I trusted you. You gave me more than enough because I gave you my word that I would use everything you trusted me with for all of your children. Thank you for never giving up on me.

To my daughter: I cannot believe I can love a person I've never seen so much. You changed my life. I apologize for being incarcerated when God blessed us with you and when God called you home. The second I heard I was going to be a father, that was the best day of my life. You were an answered prayer when I did not know how to pray yet. I always dreamed of having my own family. Before you, I thought the streets were my family. When I heard about your death, I was so heartless at the time and numb because of all the people I watched die it did not impact me at all. It took years before I understood what I lost. When I saw people close to me raising their own daughters, that's when I realized what your loss meant. That day, I promised to be the father you deserved. I could not give you the honor of having a father you could be proud of during your short time on Earth, but I gave you my word that you would be able to look down at your father and smile. All of this has been for you. The only true apology is a changed behavior. You changed my life. Every time I've pushed myself to become a better man than I believed I could be, you were my motivation. Thank you for not only being my daughter but also for being my Angel.

I want to thank my mother. When I say my mother, of course, I mean the Queen who brought me into the world, but I also mean all the mothers who looked after me during different stages of my life. My mother is unbelievably amazing in so many ways. Thank you for teaching me to never stop, instilling a deep sense of integrity and resilience in me, making me strong, and molding me into a man who would be strong enough to stand on my own two feet against the entire world. We both came into a rough world, but we not only survived, we also made the world better for people coming behind us. You don't know this, but my very first program was a replica of the work you did in the prison system while you were in college. My first mentoring program was based on things you told me about the programs you were in as a child. You paved the way for this. You raised me to always respect my elders and appreciate everything people do for me. I also want to thank Ms. Cumberlander, Ms. Johnson, and Ms. Reese. I grew up much younger than any child should. When I was in the world without my family, you all made yourselves my family. Even though I was a drug dealer and criminal, you saw the good in me. You raised me around your own children, and you knew how bad of an influence I could have been on them. You were so upset with me at times when I would get arrested and then go right back to the streets, but you did not throw me away. I did not have as much time with my mother as most children do, but I was blessed with multiple amazing mothers who stepped in.

I have so many people to thank. Karla Winfrey, words cannot express what you mean to me. You saw more in me than I saw in myself. You always told me I would be a teacher. I guess we can say you might be on to something. You took me under your wing, showed me a world I did not know existed, used your name to open doors in my life, and spoke life into me.

Mr. Yokely, you were not only my attorney but you were also the uncle I never had. You opened the doors of your firm for me to use it like an office when I needed it. You used your reputation to lift mine when everyone saw me as a convicted felon and nothing else.

Mr. Brown, I miss you, brother. You took time to lift me, mold me, and teach me everything you learned while building one of the largest empires and impressive legacies of any Black man in the country.

Minister Poole, you allowed me to come back into the same neighborhood where I caused so much damage and let me teach youth Bible study when other churches protested me. You helped me believe God had a place for me.

Pastor Durly, you saw a man who did horrible things because I was in a horrible position but who could be different if he just had a chance and then gave me that chance. Both of you baptized me because the first time, I did not fully understand the commitment I made to God, and I will always be grateful to you.

Dr. C. T. Vivian, your presence in my life set a bar for greatness I have always measured myself against. I watched you be the man the stories were written about, and you did it when no one was there to see you.

Dr. Jones, you saw a young man who wanted to help correct the problems I caused by investing in youth who grew up in homes we directly impacted with our drugs. You taught me how to take my life experiences and make them life lessons. While I mentored the youth, you mentored me.

Dr. Weldon, I was fresh out of jail myself when I told you I wanted to help other men and women coming home make the same changes I made. You believed in me so much, you trusted me to manage an entire wing of the correctional facility you oversaw and allowed me to invest in the people there.

Dr. Whylly, thank you for walking in your purpose and fighting to create change in a system that needed to be changed, and allowing me to be a part of that change.

Mr. Quinlan, thank you for not only believing in my dreams but also supporting me so we could make them happen. Your presence in my life truly changed it.

Mr. Matlock, you made my dreams into a strategy by using your wisdom to empower my purpose.

Mr. Hall, I was ordered to take your class by the courts; it was either prison or school. I am so grateful for that opportunity because you taught me so much and then stayed in my life to make sure I had someone to call when I needed it.

Commissioner Washington, you believed in what we could do together, and you pushed until we created systems that changed the quality of life for every youth in an entire county by making sure they had access to critical resources and a real opportunity to use them.

Commissioner Hall, you have lifted and believed in me from day one and given me the strength to keep going when I didn't have it.

State Representative Gillard, your heart for this work has encouraged me in more ways than you will ever know. It has been a privilege to serve our brothers and sisters behind the wall with you.

District Attorney Johnson, your passion lit a flame under me, and I could not ask for a better partner to fight alongside.

Dr. Taylor, you showed me what it means to love every single student in an entire school district and serve them like they are our only student.

To my brothers: I would not be who I am now without you. KK and Mike, you taught me how to be a man and made sure I survived in the streets. I was blessed to be born in the right neighborhood and get connected with you. Kool Aid and Kerby, everything I do you should be proud of because you motivated me to grow and showed me what was possible. Kerby, none of this would have happened without you—none of it. Mon, you have been my brother since the day we met, and that will never change. Mark and Merrill, I can barely remember before we lived across the street from each other, and I truly look at you like my brothers. Brandon, from day one, you've been authentic and solid. Kanaii Montinez Robinson, I would not be alive today if it wasn't for you. You taught me how to survive in the streets, how to thrive, and molded me into the man I am now. I remember holding your hand and asking God to spare you the first time you were shot, and he did, but the second time, I felt your soul leave your body—that was the hardest day of my life. I wish you were here with me every single day because this would be our company. To all my brothers who came out the streets with me, we were all we had, but we always had more than enough because we had each other. And to those who didn't make it out, I do this for you because you deserved a Making the Transition. Ivan, you are without a question my brother for life, and it has been an honor watching you become the man you are today. You truly have the heart of a leader who will make the world a better place. Lucas, you are a special type of brother to me because you believed in all of this from the day we met and you spoke life into me until I could see it and then used your gifts to make this happen. Frank, Eric, and Roland, you are more than my cousins—you are my backbones and I mean that. You helped me grow into a man, and when I fell, you were there. Bobby and Randy, my blood brothers, nothing is thicker than blood and it never will be.

To the Johnson sisters: thank you so much for sharing your mother with me and opening your home to me when I needed a place to call home. Ivory, you are like no one else I've ever met. I am so grateful to call you my sister because I never knew what having a sister meant until you entered my life; I learned those six letters mean everything.

To my father: I wish you could be here every single day. You were never able to see me as a man. I stopped selling drugs right when you passed. Every lesson you taught me, I held on to. You were far from perfect, but you will always be one of the realest people I've ever known. The good in you was great, and the bad made me see what type of man I would never be. I am grateful to all of you because without you, there would be no me. After my first drug-related arrest, I stayed in jail and tried to handle everything myself because I said I caused my situation. You found out and not only had my back but also respected me for standing up like a man. You said this was just a temporary stage and not to be too hard on myself because one day I'd use every lesson I learned for something bigger than I could imagine. You spoke this into existence.

Thank you to those who helped me at my final release. Judge Dempsey, thank you for seeing me as more than another case in your courtroom. Mrs. Womack, thank you for fighting for me before you had a reason to. Ms. Mckenzie, when everyone else in the courthouse saw me as another criminal, you saw more and you made them see what you did. Ms. Gipson, you were more than my bondsman—you were the person who refused to let me waste away in a jail, always told me I could be more, showed me exactly how much money I spent to be a criminal, and then challenged me to use my money wisely. All of you are the reason why I have my freedom now. You didn't give me my life back— you gave me a life, period. The man who was found guilty and should have served life stayed incarcerated. The person you believed I could be came back.

Thank you to everyone who believed in my vision of a system that could remove the toxic lessons and experiences forced on youth and then give them access to a healthy environment, a loving tribe, positive influences and exposure, powerful new tools, and life-changing resources. To every parent: thank you for believing in me enough to trust me with your precious child. To every partner: thank you so much for creating an opportunity for me to work with every last child, youth, or young adult we've reached over these last fifteen years. To the people who have supported our agency: without you, there would be no work, and I will be forever grateful to you. To each volunteer: you are the heartbeat of our agency and the reason why this vision is a reality and how we serve the people who need us.

To our youth and young adults: you deserve all of this. You are worth it and worthy. Many of you were born into situations you did not create that caused disadvantages you do not deserve, and I dedicated my life to giving you the opportunities you never had but always deserved. It has been the greatest pleasure in my life to serve you.

I never imagined I would live past the age of twenty-one. I watched so many people die selling the same drugs on the same streets as me. We chased the exact same dream because we were born into the same nightmare. I thought I would die the same way as all of my brothers. I truly believed I did not have another choice because drugs were the only way I could provide for myself. Every last one of you showed me I could be more and were my change agents. I love you and I will forever be grateful.

To Adrienne and the entire Broadleaf family: thank you for believing in me and helping us present this tool to the world.

To anyone and everyone I did not name: please do not think you are any less precious to me because you aren't.